I0699473

CRISIS IN BRAZIL

Institute of Latin American Studies
Columbia University

CRISIS
IN BRAZIL

by OCTAVIO IANNI

TRANSLATED BY
PHYLLIS B. EVELETH

COLUMBIA UNIVERSITY PRESS
NEW YORK AND LONDON 1970

OCTAVIO IANNI is Professor of Sociology
at the University of São Paulo

Copyright © 1970 Columbia University Press
Standard Book Number: 231-03221-8
Library of Congress Catalog Card Number: 74-111458
Printed in the United States of America

The Institute of Latin American Studies of Columbia University was established in 1961 in response to a national, public, and educational need for a better understanding of the nations of Latin America and a more knowledgeable basis for inter-American relations. The major objectives of the Institute are to prepare a limited number of North Americans for scholarly and professorial careers in the field of Latin American studies, to advance our knowledge of Latin America through an active program of research by faculty, by graduate students, and by visiting scholars, and to improve public knowledge through publication of a series of books on Latin America. Some of these studies are the result of research by the faculty, by graduate students, and by visiting scholars. It was also decided to include in this series translations from Portuguese and Spanish of important contemporary books in the social sciences and humanities.

During the spring semester of 1967, Dr. Octavio Ianni was Visiting Professor of Sociology (from the University of São Paulo, Brazil) at Columbia University where he taught a course on Social and Cultural Change in Brazil and a seminar on Latin American Anthropology. During that term at the Institute of Latin American Studies, he revised the draft of the Portuguese version of this present volume for publication. *Crisis in Brazil* is a translation from the Portuguese *O Colapso do Populismo no Brasil*, published in Brazil by Civilizaçaõ Brasileira in 1968.

The visiting professors and scholars who have been associated with the Institute of Latin American Studies reflect a broad spectrum of political and social thought. It is the Institute's policy in supporting their publications in English to encourage and disseminate this diversity of opinion. The publication program of the Institute of Latin American Studies is made possible by the financial assistance of the Ford Foundation.

IN MEMORY OF MY BROTHERS
ATTILIO
VITORIO
ATILIO
ARTURO
ANTONIO

PREFACE

In this book I analyze the political conditions for economic development as seen through the industrialization of Brazil. I examine the fundamental relations between the political and economic structures with the aim of clarifying the noneconomic states leading either to stagnation or to progress. In this approach, crises are considered as crucial factors. Of Brazilian crises, the Revolution of 1930 and the Coup d'Etat of 1964 are the outstanding historical episodes. The analysis will consider the political forces on the national and international levels.

This study was written between July, 1966, and May, 1967. In a major part the data and analyses presented here served as the basis for a graduate course on the Brazilian crises offered from February to March, 1967, by the Institute of Latin American Studies of Columbia University. The examination of various fundamental points will be supported by extensive documentation, for I believe that foreign and Brazilian readers alike will benefit by the introduction of important documents in seeking an interpretation of the Brazilian situation.

It is impossible to thank all who have directly or indirectly collaborated on this book. I should like to mention my friends Charles Wagley, Gabriel Cohn, and Sebastiao Simões. Lilia Guerra typed the original manuscript. Eline Maria and Aurea Maria assisted at various stages in its preparation.

OCTAVIO IANNI

Columbia University, New York
May, 1967

CONTENTS

Part I. Politics and Development

1. The Meaning of the Crises 3
2. Tensions and Conflicts 9
3. Phases of Industrialization 17
4. Agrarian Development 30

Part II. The Nationalist Epoch

5. Getulismo 47
6. Rule of the Masses in the Rural Zones 67
7. The Left and the Masses 86
8. Contradictions in the Nationalist Model 113

Part III. The New Order and Structural Dependence

9. The Coup d'Etat 127
10. The Structural Dependence 148
11. The Ideology of the Government 170
12. Dictatorship 182
13. Conclusions 196

Notes 207

Glossary 221

Abbreviations 225

Bibliography 227

Index 235

TABLES

1. Coups and Revolutions in Brazil, 1922-1964   11
2. Relevant Historical Events   14
3. Indices of Productivity, 1948-1962   25
4. Value of Industrial Production by State   27
5. Personnel, Tractors, and Plows in the States of Brazil in 1950 and 1960   34
6. Rates of Urbanization   53
7. Per Capita Income in Rural and Urban Areas, 1960   55
8. Indices of the Cost of Living, Wages, and Industrial Production   56
9. Real Minimum Salary in Rio de Janeiro   57
10. Active Economic Population in 1950 According to Principal Activities   69
11. Composition of Agricultural Labor, 1950   70
12. Population According to Occupation   72
13. Rural Unionization in Brazil   83
14. Strikes in Brazil in 1951 and 1952   96
15. Strikes in São Paulo in 1961 and 1962   96
16. Motivation for Strikes in 1952 in Brazil   97
17. Population Distribution in Rural and Urban Zones   130
18. Labor Distribution in the Three Sectors   130
19. Growth of Education   130
20. Minimum Salary in São Paulo   133
21. Direct Investments of the United States in Brazil   152
22. Foreign Capital Invested in Brazilian and Industrial Enterprises   152
23. Distribution of Foreign Capital   155
24. Foreign Investments and Financing   162

PART I

POLITICS AND DEVELOPMENT

CHAPTER 1

THE MEANING OF THE CRISES

An underdeveloped country transforms itself into an industrial society only when it attains economic and political autonomy. This autonomy only appears by means of a political and economic rupture with the traditional society and the prevailing international structures. Sometimes this rupture is complete, as in the case of Russia in 1917, China in 1949, Cuba in 1959. At other times it is partial, as was the case in the United States in 1779, in Japan with the Meiji Restoration in 1868, in Germany with Bismarck in 1862, in Brazil with Getúlio Vargas in 1930, in India with Gandhi in 1947, in Egypt with Nasser in 1952. It can be gradual or sudden, predominantly political or political and economic at the same time.

In order to interpret the nature and the meaning of such a rupture, not only as a preliminary condition but also as a basic element of development, it is necessary to be aware of the local and worldwide politico-economic structures and to define the relations between the national and international structures. Whether the break is partial and slow or complete and sudden depends upon the interrelations between these different levels. Therefore, the essence of a rupture fundamental to progress is found in the structure of both political domination and economic appropriation. A rupture that is favorable to progress can be of two types. It is revolutionary or complete when it changes the fundamental structure of the society. This always implies that a new class will rise to power, symbolizing as well as achieving the sudden break with international ties and the traditional society. On the other hand, the rupture is a reforming one when it alters certain institutions without any basic structural modification. This implies the ascension to power of other factions of the already dominant class, leading to a change in the composition of the political and economic forces.

A coup d'état in most cases is a reaction against the revolutionary or reformative solutions that are being executed or proposed. For this reason it involves the restoration and the strengthening of archaic structures. A coup d'état always inaugurates an authoritarian power and implies the formation of rigid structures for economic appropriation.

The economic, social, and political development of Brazil as characterized by rapid industrialization was the result of a series of internal and external political and economic ruptures. Generally they took place between World War I and the Coup d'Etat of 1964. The democratization of social and political relations, the expansion of the educational system, the gain of political rights and social benefits by the middle class and the working class as well as by some agricultural workers, and, in addition, other important institutional transformations were the components and the consequences of the politico-economic upheaval that occurred during this period.

The events that marked the gradual stages of the rupture in the politico-economic structures can be listed as follows: the coffee crises; nontraditional political orientation in the younger echelon of the armed forces; the appearance of working- and middle-class claims; the strengthening of antagonisms in the ruling class; World War I; the crises in world capitalism ini-

4

tiated by the Crash of 1929; the substitution of the hegemony of England, France, and Germany by the leadership of the United States; the appearance of Russia, China, and Cuba as socialist nations; the independence of India and many African nations; the appearance of Egypt and Algeria as strong and independent nations and leaders. It is clear that these occurrences were permeated by movements and countermovements resulting in revolutionary and reform agitations as well as in coups and countercoups. Considering this period as a whole, however, it unquestionably represents an era of partial and relatively slow rupture of internal and external economic and political structures. The tendencies of economic, political, and social development, as well as the accompanying crises, can be explained only when we consider the nature and the conditions of the ruptures that occurred between World War I and the Coup d'Etat of 1964.

The transition to an industrial economy in Brazil, which marks this crucial stage of development, is symbolized by the rule of the masses as the typical pattern of political organization sustaining a new power structure. The rule of the masses, different from that of political parties, is fundamental to the populist democracy that was organized slowly in the decades preceding the Coup d'Etat of 1964. This new composition of power that was created under Getúlio Vargas characterized the nationalist pattern of political action. As a consequence of it, political and cultural activities flourished, creating a different urban culture but at the same time one more authentically Brazilian. Concurrently, economic, political, and social opposition evolved, creating leftist political organizations.

The collapse of the nationalist pattern of socioeconomic development began with the government of Juscelino Kubitschek de Oliveira (1956-60), which combined in a brilliant manner the rule of the masses and the growing obligations of foreign capital. As a consequence the conflict between the nationalistic Vargas pattern of development on one side and the pattern of associated and dependent development on the other was revived in an acute manner. Moreover, it was under the Kubitschek government that the most important seeds for the future destruction of nationalistic development were sown.

For various reasons, the socioeconomic development in Brazil based on a nationalistic economy, the struggle for an independent foreign policy, the rule of the masses, and concomitantly the growing obligations toward an international capitalism were interrupted and were transported in other directions.

On the economic level the basic mechanism of transition from a policy of substitution of imports to a policy of association with foreign capital was supported by some of the following processes. First, the breakdown of trade relations occurred at the same time as the necessity to evolve a highly technical and organized industrialization in order to compete in the international market with other production centers. Second, the necessity to export (agricultural products, minerals, and manufactured articles at the same time) inherent in this transition required the elimination of protection that would allow the creation and the functioning of an industrial sector based on a policy of substitution of imports. Third, and consequently, the necessity for advanced technology resulted in a growing association with multinational big business that controlled production, research centers and laboratories, and the use of technology indispensable in international business.

On a political level the socioeconomic development exemplified by populist democracy was interrupted and reoriented.

First, economic progress had been ready to lead Brazil to an independent position with ample superiority over Latin America and Africa. Second, the rule of the masses and leftist nationalism were beginning to threaten the bourgeois political power. Third, the United States completely assumed the leadership of the capitalist world and reached a kind of Treaty of Tordesillas, a tacit understanding with the Soviet Union whereby Latin America was under the aegis of the United States.

From the historical viewpoint the dilemmas of Brazilian society can be outlined theoretically as tensions and conflicts generated by the succession and coexistence of these developmental models: export, substitution of imports, international associate, and socialist. The model of exportation of tropical products and raw materials and the importation of manufactured goods marked the economy of Brazil during the first three decades of the twentieth century. This pattern had already begun to be questioned in the second half of the previous century. However, it was with World War I and the coffee crises that it suffered the most drastic fluctuations. The Revolution of 1930 symbolized the termination of this model.

The model of substitution of imported manufactured articles was based entirely on the manipulation of the essential components of the export model. Developing rapidly from 1930 to 1962, it fluctuated in many directions and demanded a reorganization of the relations between production and the patterns of domination. In the form in which it was put into practice, that is, with a partial break with internal and external archaic structures, it paved the way for its own destruction. The succession of political crises in this period indicates the rising conflict between independent nationalism and preservation of ties with the

7

traditional society and the international politico-economic system.

The Coup d'Etat of 1964 marked the effective transition to the associate model of economic development. Implicit in the combination and regrouping of Brazilian and foreign firms is the formulation of a new concept of economic, political, cultural, and military interdependence between Latin America and the United States.

The socialist model was an actual possibility during various occasions. It developed in the beginning of the twentieth century but acquired shape and structure after the Revolution of 1930. However, it was never put into practice owing to the way in which leftist organizations interpreted the character and the meaning of industrialization in Brazil. It is undeniable that on some occasions critics set up revolutionary conditions which the leftists did not know how, or were not able, to profit by.

Finally, if we pass now to other considerations, we see that the era of rapid industrialization that took place in Brazil engendered unique politico-economic patterns. Each of these involved its special rupture and reintegration with traditional society and the international system. Thus we have reform nationalism based upon populist democracy and "technocratic" dictatorship based upon full association with foreign sectors. These are the two extremes that I would label the Brazilian revolution. The fluctuations between these two patterns are fed on the one hand by leftist struggles and on the other by contradictions inherent in reform nationalism. Moreover, the skillful combination of populist democracy with a policy of internationalizing Brazilian economy clearly exhibits those contradictions.

CHAPTER 2

TENSIONS AND CONFLICTS

Political, economic, and social events in Brazil in the twentieth century, especially after World War I, exhibited the tensions and conflicts induced by the transition to an urban-industrial culture. In contrast to the four-centuries-old agrarian culture where economic activities centered outside the country and political relations orbited about the agrarian aristocracy and the educated elite, the urban-industrial culture of the present century was organized in different political, economic, and social patterns. In the twentieth century the Brazilian people themselves emerged as a radical political class. After World War I, and on an ever-growing scale, the small urban and rural middle class and the proletariat gained importance as a political influence. One can see that the Brazilian revolution of this century is one of struggle for an increasing popular voice in political and economic discussions and decisions. The flowering of culture in Brazil, especially from the 1920s to the 1950s, shows the creation of a new national consciousness. Against this background we can view the coups, the revolutions, and the movements which marked the rises and falls in political life.

These events are not solely political nor strictly internal. They are generally manifestations of relations, tensions, and conflicts which newly formed sectors of the country established with the traditional Brazilian society and with more

9

powerful nations with which Brazil has relations. For these reasons the coups, the revolutions, and the armed movements in Brazil since World War I must be considered as politico-economic ruptures both within and outside of the country. At times these relations are not immediately visible; they cannot be confirmed empirically in a direct way. In general they have verifiable structural ties on the historic level. In such instances the breaks are manifestations of the politico-economic rupture signaling the entrance of Brazil into an urban-industrial civilization.

Let us see how the crises marking the many stages of the Brazilian revolution have developed. After that we shall see how the enlightening process in Brazil is tied to the unfolding of international events.

The period from World War I to the Coup d'Etat of 1964 was replete with armed movements, isolated acts of violence, strikes, revolts, coups, and revolutions. These events would be increased numerically if we added the tense situations and the coups and revolutions planned but not carried out by the different civil and military political groups. Table 1 shows the political and military events in the history of social struggle in Brazil between 1922 and 1964.

In many instances these political and military events were interlinked and complemented each other on various levels. For this reason it is not only possible but also convenient to analyze them as a unit. They are events that are centered around a few striking trends.

Up to 1945 the political events were tied to the necessity of reducing the political power and controlling the economic power of exporters of agricultural products and importers of manufactured goods. At the very heart of these interests lay the

TENSIONS AND CONFLICTS

TABLE 1

COUPS AND REVOLUTIONS IN BRAZIL

1922-1964

Date	Main Location	Group
1922, July 5	Rio de Janeiro	Military
1923, January 25	Rio Grande do Sul	Civil and military
1924, July 5	São Paulo	Military
1924, October 28	Rio Grande do Sul	Military
1924-1927	São Paulo – Rio Grande do Sul	Coluna Prestes
1926, October 24	Rio Grande do Sul	Naval
1930, October 3	Rio Grande do Sul	Civil and military
1932, July 9	São Paulo	Civil and military
1935, November 23	Rio de Janeiro – Natal	Civil and military
1937, November 10	Rio de Janeiro	Civil and military
1938	Rio de Janeiro	Civil and military
1945, October 29	Rio de Janeiro	Civil and military
1954, August 24	Rio de Janeiro	Civil and military
1955, November 11	Rio de Janeiro	Military and civil
1961, August	Brasília	Military and civil
1964, April 1	Brasília	Military and civil

coffee planter with his preponderant economic influence. On the one hand, there was a conflict between the traditional oligarchies and the budding urban sectors as seen in the middle class, the civil and military bureaucracy, the incipient groups of industrial entrepreneurs, and the rising proletariat. On the other hand, the political struggles were related to the conflict between the various projects of modernization, democratization, and economic development. At the base of these conflicts, however, rested the contradiction between the exportation of agricultural products and the developing industrial economy. Events up to 1945 pivoted about these confrontations.

In a large part *tenentismo* characterized this stage in Brazilian life. For all its explicitness, as well as for its chaotic

and contradictory nature, this political and ideological movement expressed important aspects of the period. Tenentismo
grew out of the following conditions: urbanization and the
growth of the middle class; a revolution in the expectations of
the middle class paralleling its quantitative growth, which
provoked a conflict between the propensity to consume and
meager income; contradictions between the structures developing from the socioeconomic transformations and the generally
rigid structures in effect; a new development in the habitual and
traditional practice of letting the military take political action
and make decisions; the inability of the rulers and dominant
groups to change the institutions, thereby broadening the con-
troversy and increasing the participation of new social groups
while maintaining authority and control of the situation; the
necessity to transform formal liberalism, inherent in patrimonial
democracy, into effective liberalism. To sum up, the political
struggles after 1922 were related to the necessity of forming a
cultural and institutional system adequate for the expanding
urban-industrial culture.

From the end of World War II, this picture changed and
became more complex. Economic and political institutions for
the development of the industrial sector already were formed.
The overthrow of the Vargas government reflected the conflict of interests and the struggles that went beyond the national
scene. Between 1945 and 1964 the salaried workers became a
more important group than ever before. After the coup d'état
against Getúlio Vargas and the *Estado Nôvo* on October 29,
1945, the Brazilian political scene included the skilled workers,
the social middle class, and groups of agricultural workers.
The aspirations for the social well-being of an ever-growing
proletariat came into play along with a numerically increasing

middle class. In addition, the claims of agricultural workers in some areas of the country were made known as they never had been before. In this period leftist political groups multiplied and the university students appeared on the scene as an active and organized political force.

This is the general outline of the different manifestations of the politico-economic break that accompanied the formation of industrial capitalism in Brazil. The more important aspects of these events will be investigated in later chapters.

This outline of political events is not complete without listing some occurrences in international politics, since they directly or indirectly affected Brazilian history. These occurrences relate to the political and economic ruptures that took place in other countries. It is important to remember that Brazil made only timid and ambiguous moves in breaking its ties with other countries. The government of Getúlio Vargas made tentative moves to do so. The government of Jânio Quadros also understood the dilemma but did not know how to handle the political moves necessary to create an independent foreign policy. For this reason the foreign politico-economic rupture which acted positively in the economic development of Brazil was principally the result of crises in international capitalism.

From a political standpoint the crises in the capitalist countries were symbolized by the two world wars. With World War I, the Crash of 1929, and World War II the leading nations underwent profound and drastic modifications in their relations with colonies and underdeveloped countries. Moreover, these events were in a greater or lesser manner responsible for the events that will be mentioned later.

Table 2 lists some of the world crises involving political and economic breaks that opened new perspectives for Brazil.

TABLE 2

RELEVANT HISTORICAL EVENTS

Year	Event	Countries Involved
1910	People's revolution	Mexico
1911	Bourgeois revolution	China
1914-18	World War I	Germany, England, France, Italy, and others
1917	Socialist revolution	Russia
1929-33	Depression	Worldwide
1930	Revolution	Brazil
1939-45	World War II	Germany, France, England, USSR, Japan, United States, and others
1947	Independence	India
1949	Socialist revolution	China
1952	Independence	Egypt
1952-53	Korean War	Korea, China, United States
1958	War of liberation	Vietnam and France
1959	Socialist revolution	Cuba
1962	Independence	Algeria
1964-	Vietnam War	North Vietnam and United States

It is to be noted that these events acted in a positive way only because they included struggles between leading nations and the weakening of some in relation to others. With regard to Brazil, the hegemony of England was opposed by Germany, France, and later by the United States. It was the United States which finally launched its supremacy and redefined its relations with Latin America as a whole and with Brazil in particular.

However, while the disputes between the major powers remained undecided and while the United States had not consolidated its predominance, new opportunities were presented for the colonies and underdeveloped countries. It is in this context that an important, perhaps decisive, stage occurred in the industrialization of Brazil. The transition to an urban-industrial society, dynamic since World War I, depended to a great extent on international contradictions and crises. In a historical perspective this tendency was examined carefully by Alan K. Manchester.

The first rival to threaten Britain's position in a serious way was Germany. As early as 1873 German tonnage was threatening to displace the United States, which held third place among foreign nations trading with Brazil, while the consul at Santos, a British stronghold, was complaining that the German crews were better trained, made a better appearance, and were far more sober than their English rivals. Shippers, to his distress, were beginning to prefer German and Norwegian boats, as rumor had it that they took better care of the cargo and charged lower rates. By 1885 German tonnage to Brazil was rivalling the French and by 1912 it was second only to England. . . .

The cataclysm of 1914 eliminated Germany as a rival in the South American republic; and yet it prepared the way for another competitor which was to succeed where others had failed. Until 1914 the United States was never a serious contender for economic preeminence in Brazilian markets, shipping, or investments. . . .

Great Britain, however, has never made a question of maintaining its early supremacy in the field of Brazilian exportations: it is primarily interested in Brazil as a market for English goods, not a supplier of raw materials for home consumption. . . .

Thus despite the occasional warning voiced by British consuls, the United States figured as a minor competitor of England until the World War, when it supplanted Great Britain as the principal supplier of the South American republic. The failure of England to maintain its traditional position during the years following 1914 was merely the natural result of war conditions and, to the Britisher, a temporary eclipse which would be rectified at the proper moment. Consequently, the real struggle for supremacy came after 1918. . . .

Thus by the end of 1929 the United States was successfully rivalling Great Britain in the buying and selling markets of Brazil.

On the other hand, in the fields of shipping and investments, English preeminence was still virtually unchallenged. In 1926 the tonnage of vessels flying the British flag was almost twice as large as that of its nearest competitor, Germany. In investments, of the estimated two billion, five hundred million dollars of foreign capital invested in Brazil in 1929 half was British. In 1927 there was four times as much British as American money invested in Brazil, and over one and one-half times as much as all other foreign capital combined. In two of the three traditional fields of British interest in the South American republic, England was still preeminent at the end of the last decade.[1]

Thus little by little Brazil passed from the sterling bloc to the dollar bloc. This tendency was heightened after 1930. According to studies of Jordan Young, there are indications that American interests were implicated in Brazil in the Revolution of 1930.

The United States government entered the military scene late in the campaign as a result of a State Department decision on October 22 to place an embargo on the sale of arms and munitions to rebel forces.[2]

CHAPTER 3

PHASES OF INDUSTRIALIZATION

It is indisputable that the industrialization of Brazil occurred because of changes in its relations with other countries. The internal economic, social, and political conditions that formed the effective bases for the developmental spurts in industry became dynamic only because of the oscillation and rupture of ties between Brazil and England, Germany, France, the United States, and other countries.

For this reason the history of industrialization in Brazil is at the same time a history of the foreign relations of Brazil with the leading world powers. Actually the progress of the manufacturing industry emphasizes and is interlocked with Brazilian and world history. Brazilian history is based in, and illustrated again by, the history of capitalism. To a great extent the former is a function of the latter.

It is in this sense that we can reconstruct the stages in the formation of the industrial sector as a dynamic nucleus for economic development. The evolutionary phases can be reconstructed only as the specific relations between the Brazilian economy and the foreign systems with which Brazil happened to be linked at the time. Three principal stages in the industrial development of Brazil can be recognized.

POLITICS AND DEVELOPMENT

The first stage developed inside the colonial economy. Up to 1930 the economic life of the country was organized after the export model. Coffeegrowing was the predominant productive activity, defining the character of the economic structure as a function of exports. It symbolized the developmental pattern in this period. The crises and the up and downs in the coffee market opened many opportunities in the Brazilian economy that created incentives for craftsmanship and the production of manufactured goods. When the profits from coffee were not sufficient for the purchase of traditionally imported manufactured goods, the artisans and small manufacturers worked harder to take care of the demand at least partially. As a consequence, the existent enterprises had more business, which led to the creation of new firms.

This extremely crucial period in the formation of industries in Brazil has been discussed by Caio Prado, Jr., Roberto C. Simonsen, and Celso Furtado, as well as by other historians, sociologists, and political scientists. They have explained the causes and effects of the mechanism of *socialization of losses* in the coffee sector. Celso Furtado has presented a brilliant interpretation of this dynamic process and, in a great part, of the development of industry.

The process worked as follows: The crisis in the coffee market from 1929 to 1933, as with crises typical of a colonial economy, came from outside the country. It first manifested itself as a drop in the profits of the coffee planters. The drop came from a reduction in consumption or a lowering of prices in the external market, which amounts to the same thing, producing a sharp decrease in the planters' profits. So that the planters would not abandon coffeegrowing, the Brazilian government depreciated the value of the currency. Thus in terms of Brazilian currency the coffee planters continued to receive approximately the same amount of income. In this manner the decrease in their profits was lessened, allowing them to continue working the plantations. As is obvious, at the same time the import capacity of the country was reduced owing to the high exchange rate. In this way new stimuli were created for the incipient secondary sector of the Brazilian economy — industry.

The fact that coffee production had continued to expand after the crisis and the circumstance by which the coffee planters had become accustomed to the protective plans directed by the government resulted in a large degree from the support of the monetary return from exports. The coffee producer was not concerned that the accumulation of coffee stocks was being financed with foreign loans or through the expansion of credit. The decision to continue financing an accumulation of stocks without foreign resources, whatever the repercussion on the balance of payments, resulted in consequences that could not be suspected at the time. The monetary demand thus was maintained on a relatively elevated level in the export sector. This fact, together with the sharp rise in the cost of imports (a result of the depreciation in exchange), the existence of an idle capacity in some industries of the internal Brazilian market, and the fact that there already existed a small nucleus of capital goods industries in the country, explains the quick rise in industrial production, which became the principal dynamic factor in the realization of income.[1]

It was in this period and in this manner that metamorphosis of agrarian capital to industrial capital occurred. In the first stage of industrialization the capital that went into manufacturing came from the coffee crop. Directly and indirectly coffee raising nurtured the initial stage of industrialization. Afterwards this process became somewhat more complex when foreign capital and capital from internal savings began to be used. In every circumstance, however, coffee was the ultimate support of business. If it is true that the differentiation of the Brazilian economy is inspired in part by the conviction of entrepreneurs that not all capital should be subject to the risks of the coffee economy, it is also true that coffee is a point of reference that is always safe. Experience gained from this activity, besides engaging the government in connections and confidences with foreign nations, always gave coffee the role of the great bondsman. For this reason, on the structural level agricultural capital was the foundation of industrial capital. On the effective level of everyday lending and borrowing, there were other sources of capital for the industrial sector. Moreover, it is important not to confuse the two levels or to consider them as a single dimension.

The second stage in the industrial development of Brazil consisted in the application of means destined to reconcile the diversification and expansion of the industrial sector. Here one finds the Revolution of 1930, the Estado Nôvo instituted in 1937, the nationalist pattern and its variants, and populist democracy. In general terms, the period from 1930 to 1964 was a time of forming the model of substitution of imports. The experiences of Vargas and his methods deeply marked this phase, so much so that the model of the Economic Commission for Latin America (ECLA) in its first stage (1948-58) was in a large part a codification of the developmental experiences of Mexico, Chile, Brazil, and other South American countries. According to Raul Prebisch:

The Economic Commission (ECLA) was set up on an experimental basis for three years, and in 1951, as the end of this period approached, there were very powerful forces interested in its elimination from Latin America. I knew this very well when I accepted the responsibility that was given to me. I had been told so harshly by an eminent Latin American who was very much in tune with the ideas prevalent in those times. "You are wasting your time," he said, "since the OAS is there to do what has been entrusted to ECLA."

I do not believe I have wasted it. The decisive battle occurred in our fourth set of meetings in Mexico in the middle of 1951. I was almost ready for defeat. Chile, which had fought with enthusiasm for the creation of ECLA was almost alone. Two items were decisive at this moment: (a) the position of Brazil, which, after certain initial vacillations, vigorously took up the defense of ECLA after its delegation received a personal cable from President Vargas; (b) the resolved attitude of Mexico. Together with Chile, these countries organized the resistance to the point of causing a complete change.

Some weeks later in Rio I was to meet President Vargas accompanied by Celso Furtado. There have been few times in my life when I have had a conversation so categorical and precise. In a few words the President explained to me the reason for his attitude: the necessity of an independent organ in the hands of Latin Americans.[2]

Between 1930 and 1964 a vigorous industrial sector was created in Brazil. In this period the state became the most important center for decision-making in economic policy. This was true to such a degree that public authority not only formulated and oriented the economic policies but also came to execute some of the points in the developmental programs. The creation of the National Economic Development Bank (BNDE) in 1952, the Brazilian Petroleum Corporation (Petrobrás) in 1953, and the Northeast Development Authority (SUDENE) in 1959 shows the directions in which the government rushed headlong to make a more dynamic national economy.

It is clear that the applications of the model of substitution of imports are not seen when following a single directive nor when based on a clear and preconceived idea. There were a series of crises in this period that were due to improvisations. In spite of everything, the export model continued and played a part in the political schemes, especially in economic policy. Yet the actual manner in which substitution of imports was put into practice created the foundations for a third pattern in economic development.

The third stage of industrial development in Brazil should be identified with the model of associate development or internationalization of the Brazilian economy, specifically, internationalization of the industrial sector. In practice this pattern was always present to some degree in the Brazilian economic structure. During the period of the dominance of the export model, foreign capital already was directed toward areas of transportation, communications, production of electricity, and mining. Even before 1930 foreign loans were indispensable in order to face the periodic crises in the coffee market and the difficulties with the government budget.[3] Afterwards in the phase of the deliberate policy of substitution of imports, foreign capital appeared more and more frequently in the form of financing and investments.

The stage at which the conditions of economic development in Brazil came to depend completely on the direct and indirect, visible and disguised association between Brazilian and foreign capital began as a governmental policy with the Coup d'Etat of 1964. In practice the model that was destined to internationalize the Brazilian economy had already been implanted several years earlier with the *Programa de Metas* of the government of Juscelino Kubitschek. The pattern of associate development was executed at various times. On the one hand, its economic theory, which previously had been misinterpreted, was carried out completely under the Programa de Metas. On the other hand, its political theory, also previously distorted, was accomplished fully under the government of Marshal Humberto de Alencar Castello Branco. On an economic level, which is what interests us here, the policy of association and internationalization can be seen as a governmental policy in the following words of former President Juscelino Kubitschek's messages to Congress:

> There is something more that touches on general policy. Another measure to which the government gives great importance is the attraction of foreign enterprises which with their technology and their capital can give valuable aid in the construction of our industrial parks. The essential conditions for a policy to stimulate foreign capital are political exchange and monetary stability . . .
>
> A fact of great importance which occurred in 1956 was the renewed interest of foreign capitalists in the industrial development of Brazil. This interest was due principally to the climate of confidence which the new administration succeeded in establishing abroad. The truth is that today the concept of Brazil abroad has been transformed entirely and our country is taking first place in the market competing for foreign capital.[4]

Whether in supplementing foreign exchange credits necessary for the financing of federal projects or in lending support to private, domestic enterprises in obtaining loans from abroad, the responsible authorities advanced various modalities of action, careful, however, of the prospects of our medium- and long-term balance of payments in order to avoid a disproportionate foreign obligation.

One of those modalities of action consisted in attracting direct foreign investments by means of encouraging incentives to establish certain industries, as, for example, the automobile industry. In other cases we fell back upon the official entities for credit, both domestic and foreign — the International Bank for Reconstruction and Development, the Export-Import Bank of Washington, the Instituto Mobiliare Italiano, the Assurance Crédit de France, and some others — by means of opening bank credits in favor of the National Economic Development Bank or guaranteed by them. In raising foreign resources it is not unusual to call upon a seller's credit or the granting of long- and medium-term credits by the supplier of machinery, whether or not guaranteed by the government of the exporting country.

In this aspect the results have been satisfactory in relation to the on-going projects. For $80 million registered in 1955 with the Superintendency of Money and Credit (SUMOC) as risk capital, in 1956 and 1957 $302 million and $261 million were registered respectively. In 1958 the registration was raised to $397 million. As for direct investments, these figures were raised by $31 million in 1955, $56 million in 1956, $109 million in 1957, and $104 million in 1958.[5]

As a result of these briefly summarized stages, especially the deliberate policy of substitution of imports, a vigorous industrial sector was established in Brazil. In addition to its specific importance, it served as a dynamic nucleus affecting other sectors of the economy and causing complementary reactions. A picture of the progress of industrialization and the functioning of other sectors of the economy can be seen in Table 3.

As industrialization developed and the domestic economic structure became differentiated, the state each time grew in importance. It became the main center for decisions on the domestic level. By means of tax benefits, loans, technical assistance, and as co-signer, federal authorities and governmental agencies provided incentives and orientation to pioneer investments. Moreover, the government had already been taking a full part in decisions and responsibilities during the period of the predominance of the export pattern. The coffee economy

PHASES OF INDUSTRIALIZATION

TABLE 3

INDICES OF PRODUCTIVITY

1948-1962

(Base: 1949 = 100)

Sector	1948	1950	1952	1954	1956	1958	1960	1962[a]
Agriculture	95.7	101.5	111.7	120.5	126.7	141.3	156.1	177.1
Industry	90.6	111.4	124.4	146.7	173.5	213.2	264.8	316.0
Commerce	96.2	104.1	122.5	136.7	142.7	171.1	197.8	217.8
Transportation and communication	92.3	108.0	126.4	147.7	157.5	176.7	219.1	256.2
Government	97.6	102.4	107.4	112.6	118.1	123.9	130.0	136.3
Service	97.1	103.0	109.4	116.1	123.3	130.9	139.0	147.6
Rents	96.4	103.5	111.0	119.3	128.2	137.8	148.0	158.8

Source: Centro das Contas Nacionais, Fundação Getúlio Vargas. Cf. *Revista Brasileira de Economia*, Ano 17, No. 1 (Rio de Janeiro, March, 1963), p. 14.
[a] Preliminary estimate.

saw government participation in the national economy to an ever-increasing degree.

Considered as a whole, the participation of government institutions in the economic field can be classified in two stages, corresponding to two distinct orientations. Partly the two stages represent two successive phases in the evolution of government intervention. However, it is important to realize that they coexist as ambiguities in the Brazilian economic structure.

In phase one, which corresponds to a perfectly shaped orientation, the state acts from the necessity of preserving certain levels of income and employment in determined sectors of production. It acts as regulator of production and creates means of protection for sectors with a threatened level of income due to internally or externally caused disorders and crises. The institutes of coffee, salt, pine, chocolate, *mate*, sugar, and alcohol were all entities created with the immediate object of protecting these sectors from sharp fluctuations in income and employment such as were caused by disturbances in production or distribution. The most notable case for its importance in the domestic economy is that of coffee. In this the means formulated by the organ of coffeegrowers and put into practice by government authorities were continually refined because of the great importance of this sector for the preservation of employment and income levels and also for the domestic economy as a whole . . .

In phase two the state actively enters into the various spheres of economic life, collaborating, motivating, and creating wealth. In this class the National Steel Company (CSN), the Amazon Economic Development Authority (SPVEA), the São Francisco Valley Company, the Bank of the Northeast of Brazil (BNB), Petrobrás, Eletrobrás, the Northeast Development Authority (SUDENE), the National Economic Development Bank (BNDE), the Plano Salte, the Programa de Metas, and the Plano Trienal are outstanding. With varying degrees of success all these enterprises were put into practice with a different motive from that which had inspired the previous phase. Now the government has pledges to fulfill in regional and even over-all programs of development. Stimulated by domestic and foreign tensions, the state assumed increased functions that were destined to give energy and direction to the productive forces.[6]

Each phase corresponds to the dominance of one or the other economic policy. Basically, at first the state was eminently conservative, but increasingly its activity became dynamic and reforming. However, the increasing federal participation in the economy, as well as the modernization of techniques of diagnosis, formulation, execution, and control of the economy, did not advance to the point of allowing the domination and the elimination of inequalities and struc-

PHASES OF INDUSTRIALIZATION

TABLE 4

VALUE OF INDUSTRIAL PRODUCTION BY STATE

(Percentage distribution)

State	1907	1920	1938	1958
Federal District [a]	33.1	20.8	14.2	11.4
São Paulo	16.5	31.5	43.2	55.0
Rio Grande do Sul	14.9	11.0	10.7	7.7
Rio de Janeiro	6.7	7.4	5.0	6.6
Paraná	4.9	3.2	1.8	3.1
Minas Gerais	4.8	5.5	11.3	5.6
Pernambuco	4.0	6.8	4.2	2.8
Bahia	3.2	2.8	1.7	1.5
Pará	2.7	1.1	0.7	0.6
Amazonas	2.0	0.1	0.2	0.3
Santa Catarina	2.0	1.9	1.8	2.1
Alagoas	1.0	1.6	0.7	0.5
Maranhão	0.7	0.7	0.3	0.2
Sergipe	0.6	1.2	0.6	0.2
Mato Grosso	0.5	0.2	0.2	0.3
Ceará	0.4	0.8	0.9	0.6
Paraíba	0.4	1.1	0.8	0.6
Goiás	0.2	0.1	0.2	0.3
Piauí	0.1	0.2	0.1	0.1
Rio Grande do Norte	0.1	0.6	0.4	0.3
Espírito Santo	0.1	0.7	0.2	0.2
Total	98.9	99.3	99.2	100.0

Sources: J. Jobim, *Brazil in the Making* (New York, The Macmillan Co., 1943); Instituto Brasileiro de Geografia e Estatística, *Produção Industrial Brasileira* (Rio de Janeiro, IBGE, 1958). Table organized by Juarez Rubens Brandão Lopes, "Desenvolvimento e Mudança Social (Formação da Sociedade Urbano-Industrial no Brasil)" (São Paulo, 1966), MS.
[a] Known today as the State of Guanabara, mainly the city of Rio de Janeiro.

tural distortions. The development of the national economy can be witnessed on various levels. Inflation, for example, with techniques of forced savings, opened the way for the analysis of class relations and the generation of capital. Exodus from the country to the city, on the other hand, caused problems which revealed the social and human dimensions of industrialization and urbanization in Brazil.

A look at Table 4 will give an idea of the industrial evolution according to regional manifestations for half a century of economic activities: 1907, 1920, 1938, and 1958. It can be observed that economic progress is not homogeneous, nor does it necessarily show tendencies toward an equal growth in all states. At least the equalization of the indices of development are not yet visible at the stages that already have taken place.

Actually Table 4 shows progressions and regressions when the data are considered together. However, upon closer examination a progressive dominance of one center — the hegemony of São Paulo over the other states — can be observed. As a growth center São Paulo attracts more benefits of industrialization than it diffuses out. There is a type of internal colonialism that the national and regional programs could not limit. The activities of the majority of the regional agencies that were created especially to stimulate the local economies did not succeed in lessening the regressive effects inherent in the concentration and centralization of capital. Perhaps the programs had facilitated the predominance of the South Central States with a center at São Paulo. This is one of the consequences of the character of industrial development in progress in Brazil. Moreover, it is an inevitable result of the succession of stages of expansion in the industrial sector.

To summarize, industrialization in Brazil examined in a historic perspective reveals the following points clearly:

a) the partial rupture and the recomposition (successively and alternately) of political and economic relations with the traditional society and foreign systems;

b) the frustration of attempts to establish an autonomous economic model of development;

c) the combination of export, substitution, and associate or international models in a heterogeneous and contradictory economic system;

d) the increasing participation of the state in controlling the economic process;

e) the transformation of the South Central States into a hegemonic nucleus in the national economy with centers at the cities of São Paulo, Rio de Janeiro, and Belo Horizonte;

f) the formation of popular movements as political and ideological structures which kept government policy oriented toward industrial development.

CHAPTER 4

AGRARIAN DEVELOPMENT

The moment that the first industrial nuclei are created, a conflict is established between the city and the country. Even if it is true that the genesis of the industrial sector lies in the agrarian sector, that one grows out of the other, this does not mean that their relations are harmonious and always positive. Nor could they be, since changes in the economic structure affect interrelationships with production and power. The actual technical conditions for capital formation are varied, favoring distinct rhythms in the flow of capital.

In any case, in each stage of industrial development a definite pattern is found interlocking the city with the country and the agrarian society with industrial society. The way in which capital is raised and distributed, the movement of workers in the labor market, the technical and organizational conditions of production, the access to the instruments of authority — all these are implied in the relations and antagonisms between the agrarian and industrial sectors.

However, one must emphasize a reciprocal and ever-increasing dependency on the part of both sides. Because of the very dynamics of economic, political, and social life, the city and the country are persuaded to support each other in the solution or to adjust themselves to their differences. One must keep in mind not only the multiplying effects of one sector on another but also the complementary nature inherent in economic organization. According to Pei-kang Chang, who was dedicated to the study of economic development concerning the relations between agriculture and industry:

> Interdependence between the economic activities carried out by one agricultural country and another industrial country is no less narrow or profound than the interdependence of economic, agricultural, and industrial activities within the same country.[1]

This interdependence can be demonstrated at various levels. In the previous chapter we saw how dynamic and at the same time negative relations were established between coffee raising and the budding industrial sector. In addition, the data presented in Table 3 in the same chapter demonstrated that agriculture rose 77 percent between 1949 and 1962. If we exclude the export products whose tangible worth grew only 27 percent in those years, we discover that products for internal consumption increased 90 percent. Yet it is to be noted that the Brazilian population grew around 40 percent between 1950 and 1960, and less than 80 percent between 1940 and 1960.[2] Moreover, the agricultural sector showed symptoms of transformation or development that could not be ignored.

It is a fact that in this same period productivity in the industrial sector increased 216 percent. Moreover, it should be remembered that this was the period of intense mobilization of resources and incentives, public and private, domestic and foreign, in order to give energy and diversification to industry. In this regard *confisco cambial* was an instrument for transferring resources from coffee exportation to industry. In addition, it is important to take into consideration that the rhythm and volume of formation of agrarian capital are necessarily different from those of industrial capital. Natural conditions and seasonal fluctuations are limitations that never, or rarely, affect the industrial sector. For this reason less time is needed for the flow of industrial capital. Moreover, the amount of capital mobilized can be larger as a result of greater organization of businesses. To sum up, industrial capital avails itself of better conditions for expansion, which leads it to acquire ever-increasing advantages over agrarian capital. These structural conditions for the formation of capital in the two basic sectors of the economy cannot be underestimated if we wish to understand the Brazilian situation.

The relative retardation in the agrarian sector must not be considered indicative of the absence of progress or even of significant changes. The rural exodus, for example, is not a unilateral fact arising from the attraction of the city and its industries. It is related also to the changes in the technical and social conditions of production in several of the agricultural regions. This can be seen in the following analysis by José Francisco de Camargo:

> In spite of the fact that we can see only partially a relationship between the mechanization of agriculture and improved organization on the farms, we cannot help but infer the existence of interdependence in some regions between the rural exodus and the technical progress in agriculture. . . .
>
> Technical innovations for the preparation and planting of the land, improved transportation of agricultural products, and a sharp increase in the rural population all worked positively to stimulate the rural exodus in our country.[3]

However, we can draw upon another indicator. A detailed examination of the agrarian sector reveals that the use of fertilizers and tractors is augmenting continually, indicating modernization in the agricultural productive process. The causes of the rural exodus, together with the data concerning the increase in the use of tractors in Brazilian agriculture, demonstrate the expansion of capitalism in rural areas. In other words, interdependence between the industrial and agricultural sectors continues to develop. This process is neither uniform nor universal in Brazilian agrarian society. It is perfectly delineated, however, in the states of São Paulo, Rio Grande do Sul, Minas Gerais, Rio de Janeiro, and Espírito Santo. In these states the increase in the number of tractors occurred simultaneously with the reduction in, or the relative stabilization of, the population engaged in agriculture. Moreover, even in the states of the Northeast, where the archaic structures of production are more evident, one can see a small scattering of tractors. However, the use of the plow increases much more rapidly in this region, since the plow is an agricultural implement that is more accessible to the mass of workers from a financial and technical point of view.

These tendencies are indicated in Table 5 and can be enlarged upon. There are some developments in the agrarian society in various regions of the country which show progress and profound change in capitalist enterprise in rural areas. This has been pointed out by Paulo Schilling in a study on the expansion of agrarian capitalism in Rio Grande do Sul.

Rice, with its large-scale plantings, initiated in Rio Grande the type of agricultural exploitation designated by Americans as "plantations." This was the beginning of the penetration of capitalism into rural Rio Grande. For the first time substantial investments, salaried workers on a large scale, agricultural machines, and modern methods of cultivation were employed. It caused a real "rush"

33

TABLE 5

States and Territories	Personnel 1950	Personnel 1960	Tractors 1950	Tractors 1960	Plows 1950	Plows 1960
Rondônia	4,678	4,188	5	8	11	7
Acre	15,905	28,938	5	16	33	18
Amazonas	80,705	166,259	10	24	73	32
Roraima	2,444	3,225	2	1	31	12
Pará	219,985	329,815	33	194	219	202
Amapá	2,785	4,194	6	23	14	35
Maranhão	368,625	928,801	16	41	180	118
Piauí	206,307	355,187	20	59	499	1,403
Ceará	498,803	816,720	32	316	821	1,305
Rio Grande do Norte	234,737	296,494	17	246	414	305
Paraíba	434,143	544,797	62	361	532	611
Pernambuco	879,844	1,258,479	142	999	3,902	5,861
Alagoas	274,985	364,390	35	296	2,683	5,608
Sergipe	154,721	243,396	45	96	811	666
Bahia	1,282,771	1,857,771	82	575	4,647	5,294
Minas Gerais	1,868,657	2,076,829	763	5,024	73,968	93,040
Serra dos Aimorés	33,276	176,646		8	4	43
Espírito Santo	272,992	269,041	58	490	1,666	2,458
Rio de Janeiro	276,730	240,853	457	1,469	12,020	12,314
Guanabara	16,541	18,937	58	123	258	171
São Paulo	1,531,664	1,683,038	3,819	28,101	224,947	286,580
Santa Catarina	370,912	619,989	41	1,049	41,029	81,259
Paraná	507,607	1,276,854	280	4,996	30,405	82,324
Rio Grande do Sul	1,071,404	1,277,390	2,245	16,675	312,001	440,467
Mato Grosso	86,279	184,340	50	997	1,118	5,386
Goiás	299,334	492,745	89	1,299	1,973	6,388
Federal District (Brasília)		2,385		7		23
Brazil (total)	10,996,834	15,521,701	8,372	63,493	714,259	1,031,930

Source: Serviço Nacional de Recenseamento. Cf. Instituto Brasileiro de Georgrafia e Estatística, *Anuario Estatístico do Brasil* (Rio de Janeiro, IBGE, 1965), p. 90.

that spread throughout the rural area because, as will be verified with wheat, the workers in the rice fields were in the majority not traditional farmers but citizens from all occupational categories. . . .

Wheat production in the state, which had remained practically stationary at 140,000 tons in 1922 and 162,488 tons in 1946, rose in ten years at an accelerated pace, reaching 992,230 tons in 1956. (This figure represents the total production, including about 10 percent for seed and local consumption in the growing areas where there are dozens of small mills that are not supervised by the S.E.T.)

How should one explain this extremely rapid progress that was without precedent in Brazil, perhaps in the world? How was it possible to increase wheat production six times in scarcely ten years while facing constantly adverse conditions in the agronomic and economic sectors?

Men with pioneer spirit, plus capital and credit, plus agronomic science, plus tens of thousands of agricultural machines, plus the capacity of our peasant — yesterday a farm peon, today the driver of a tractor or a mechanic — they created this wonder. Continuing the transformation begun with rice, wheat has revolutionized the *gaúcho* countryside today. The capitalist penetration into the rural areas is a victorious event. Capital applied to wheat agriculture, considering machines, installations, farms created from private means (without financing), and private lands, must run into a figure of ten billion cruzeiros. The inventory of agricultural machines, tractors, and harvesters runs around 10,000 units. The number of planters according to the 1957 census of the Ministry of Agriculture was 131,000, 95 percent of which are small producers. The number of salaried workers on the mechanized farms also reaches several tens of thousands.[4]

To offer a complete picture of the Brazilian agrarian society as far as the organization of production is concerned, we must realize that traditional technology and institutions exist together with and alongside the modern organization. In an exploratory study designed to evaluate the technological development of

Brazilian agriculture, Rui Miller Paiva and William H. Nichols (1965) arrived at the conclusion that the country could be divided into three principal regions: (1) a region of extensive agriculture and generally primitive methods, (2) a region of intensive agriculture and generally primitive methods, (3) a region of agriculture of a more commercial nature with more organized methods. In this last group are included areas in the south-central part of the country with the following characteristics:

> The agriculture in this last class is more of a business enterprise in the sense that the grower depends less on natural resources and more on his own organization. The farmer buys a greater amount of fertilizers, machines, fuel, feed, vaccines, etc., in order to be able to produce. Consequently, he is obligated to watch more carefully price fluctuations and markets in order to be able to sell what he produces with a profit.[5]

The agrarian structures are neither absolutely rigid nor absolutely closed. From the point of view of economic development based upon industrialization, the agrarian society should undergo more drastic and accelerated changes. In fact, the discord between the primary agrarian sector and the secondary industrial sector was and is provoking friction and waste at an international economic level. However, it is well to recognize that the agrarian structures are not autonomous nor immune to change. Actually they are integrated into broader national and international structures. These are the bonds which establish the conditions for change as well as stability.

The tenacity of the traditional agrarian structures, economic as well as political, to a great extent arises from the fact that the rural world is deeply influenced by the export model as an organizational model of economy. In other words, the friction and incongruities between the functioning of the agrarian sector and the functioning of the industrial sector do not depend only on the individualities of each sector. In actuality they depend upon the interplay and conflict of interests relative to the appropriation and formation of capital. Structurally (and, appropriately, historically) the contradictions between both sectors are governed by the fact that the agrarian sector is conditioned by the export model. The agrarian segment of Brazil continues to turn to sources outside the country as those most important for the raising of capital. In addition, the decision-making centers affecting rural Brazil remain overseas. In a certain sense the Brazilian agrarian sector is found still to be dominated by the colonial pattern, while the industrial sector needed to achieve a partial break with this pattern in order to consolidate itself. Even more, only the secondary sector can be created as a result of transitory weakening due to crises, wars, and revolutions of colonial capitalism. In this area are found the reasons for the antagonisms between the city and the country. But it is exactly in this area that we discover the fundamentals for conciliation and integration between the rural world and the urban-industrial world.

These are the principal reasons why the agrarian society does not modernize on a scale that is indispensable to the requirements of industrial development. It is important to realize that industrial development, which depends upon and requires social change in the agrarian world, is itself a determinant. We are dealing with industrial development that is immersed in a project of international economic development of an independent type. Moreover, we are concerned with the model of industrialization that was put into practice between 1930 and

1964, especially the nationalist model, which depended upon a growing redefinition of foreign relations and of relations with the traditional society.

It was in this period that the first signals of political organization were manifested among the agricultural workers. The tensions and the conflicts inherent in the exploitative production operative in the rural areas could no longer be controlled by traditional techniques of favors, pressure, and violence. Associations, leagues, and unions of agricultural workers appeared. One of the first organizations was created in the state of Pernambuco in 1955. In 1963 the Rural Worker's Statute (*Estatuto do Trabalhador Rural*) was promulgated. Twenty years previously in 1943 the Labor Laws (*Consolidação das Leis do Trabalho*) had been promulgated. In both cases work relations were formalized in terms logically consistent with the capitalist labor market in the spirit of the nationalist model.

When the model for autonomous development began to be abandoned, especially with the economic policy put into practice under the administration of Juscelino Kubitschek, the colonial pattern of organization in the Brazilian agrarian sector shifted to associate itself in a new way with the international pattern of economic development. In such a manner the rural society and the industrial society joined together again in establishing new obligations with foreign sectors. By this association the antagonisms between the city and the country were minimized, but this does not mean that they were eliminated. It only means that the depth of the antagonism was reduced now that industrialization was no longer linked to a project for national and autonomous development. There was no longer the necessity for drastic domestic and foreign ruptures.

These events and the relationships they disclose are important for a proper discussion of the crucial problems of agrarian reform. In addition, they indicate why these problems have been placed in an ambiguous or confused light. Under certain circumstances the problems are unreal.

An investigation of the projects presented before Congress and the debates there and in the press reveals several important points. On a general level the argument places in confrontation two basic positions.

The first considers agrarian reform as a technique for the socialization of the productive process. This interpretation involves the acceptance of the parceling out of the latifundia as a revolutionary instrument, since this would destroy or reduce the power of the large estate owners in the most backward regions. This position is not concerned with the other side of the proposal, which would involve the creation of large contingents of small landowners. At the beginning they would be revolutionaries in their struggles for the possession of land and the weakening of the economic and political power of the latifundist. Following this they inevitably would be conservatives owing to the fact that they would become proprietors. The ownership of land weakens previous political motivations. We are concerned here with a typical model of reforming socialism based on the presupposition that growing state control of the economy and definite types of social reforms should be able to lead a country toward an economically and politically socialistic organization.

The second position considers agrarian reform as a technique for logically organizing the agricultural economy. In this case modernization of labor relations is sought and the abandonment of traditional exploitative patterns symbolized by the voucher, the company store, and physical violence. It is planned that the tensions and conflicts in the processes of production will be eliminated. Associated with this objective is the anticipation that agrarian reform will reconcile the expansion of the internal market with the industrial sector. Furthermore, these two goals, formalized processes of production and an effective internal market, can be reached as soon as the Estatuto do Trabalhador Rural is applied. In this sense the reorganization of the factors of production with the object of increasing agricultural productivity does not depend exclusively upon agrarian reform. It depends instead upon the complete and effective application of a pattern that is characteristically capitalistic in the organization of the processes of production.

Pei-kang Chang gives the following view:

Industrial development is a necessary but not sufficient condition for agricultural reform and progress, since reform and progress refer to the mechanization of agriculture and the organization of large agricultural enterprises. Industrial development is a necessary condition because agricultural machinery, chemical fertilizers, and other implements necessary for modern agriculture must be supplied by modern industry. Other than this only an appreciable increase in the income of the population resulting from industrial and commercial expansion can augment, however, in a diminishing scale, the demand for agricultural products and thus stimulate agricultural progress. But industrial development in itself is not sufficient to induce agrarian reform. It is necessary simultaneously to count on other conditions, which must occur previous to the agrarian reform itself, in order to accomplish the effective changes. Among these diverse conditions the most important are improved transportation, consolidation of agricultural enterprises, and the legal regulation of land redistribution. In this manner the reorganization of agriculture can become a reality.[6]

Even ignoring the concept of reform as a technique of socialism known as reforming socialism, some of the goals of reform are being (or can be) reached by other means. In addition to the application of labor legislation for the rural population (which is a recent element), favoring and forcing the effective commercialization of the processes of production on a greater or lesser scale, the following facts and actual processes are outstanding: rural-urban migration; expansion of the zones of influence and dominance of the industrial centers; growth of the means of communication and information; the increased consumption of machines, tools, and fertilizers on the agricultural establishments; the discrete or drastic action of SUDENE, the São Francisco Valley Hydroelectric Company (CHEVF), the São Francisco Valley Company, the Composite Commission of the Uruguay-Paraguay Basin, the National Department of Projects Against Drought (DNOCS), the Amazon Economic Development Authority (SPVEA), and the Bank of the Northeast of Brazil (BNB); and the construction of highways such as that from Brasília to Belém.

The debate over the problems listed under agrarian reform became at times ambiguous or confused. Rarely was the debate supported by an objective examination of the process of capital formation, of the technical and institutional conditions for the functioning of the society and the agrarian economy, of the antagonisms and continuities between the primary sector and the secondary and tertiary sectors. In general the "agrarian question" was expressed in terms that were fundamentally political, without a correlated analysis of the economic and sociocultural factors. Finally, rather drastic ruptures with the traditional society (essentially colonial) were proposed without the necessary corresponding and correlated ruptures in the area of foreign relations. This was the case to such a degree that Celso Furtado felt obligated to argue in detail about the question of agrarian reform in the most important "problem region" in Brazil, that is, the Northeast.

In the economy of the *caatinga* the dividing up of the land would be a shot of misery into the economy, including the possible termination of cattle raising. For the man in the street, agrarian reform means land division, elimination of the large estate owner, elimination of income from the land. Were we to do this in the caatinga, we would depopulate the region, completely disorganizing its economy, which would be a grave error. Given the ecological conditions of the caatinga and given the type of technology that is utilized there, the subdivision of lands would turn into depopulation because no man can subsist in the caatinga with a small or even medium-sized landholding. A piece of property of 25 hectares in the region can be maintained only when supplied with a source of water. In order for man to subsist, the unit for production in the caatinga must be relatively large, since the land is poor and in a fixed way one has to compensate in quantity what one lacks in quality. . . .

In the *agreste*, if one searches thoroughly, he finds lands that are extremely divided up. Any agrarian reform in this region would immediately involve a combining of these units. The agreste is poorer in certain technical aspects than the *sertão*. That is another angle of the problem on which I cannot enlarge. In the agreste a man in order to survive producing cotton cannot hold less than 10 hectares. Ten hectares for cotton and 10 more hectares for the livestock if some traction animal is needed. A productive unit in the agreste must average 20 hectares, which in this case corresponds to a large holding. . . .

Agrarian reform here will not be carried out by dividing up the land, but on the contrary by combining small farms. Whether the operation must be carried out by throwing the landowner out, estate owner or not, is a political problem and the option for one form or another does not fall to the economist.[7]

The crucial problem of agrarian society ceases to be merely and fundamentally agrarian reform. As long as production is in a capitalistic economy, agricultural progress is dependent upon the expansion of capitalistic techniques in rural areas. When we consider the given capitalistic manner of production as a base, the most logical utilization of the land depends primarily upon how the agricultural product performs in the market, and only secondarily upon the relations of production and technology. Thus the point around which the agrarian question in Brazil revolves continues to be the survival and persistence of a colonial pattern for the organization of production. As the stimuli of the domestic and international markets vary, modifications of the economic and political structures of rural Brazil can occur. On a certain level, then, the agrarian society is doubly dependent — subordinated to foreign centers of decision-making and to the already predominant functions of the industrial sector.

PART II

THE NATIONALIST EPOCH

CHAPTER 5

GETULISMO

The rule of the masses was the life and death of the nationalist model of economic development that unfolded under Getúlio Vargas. During one of the more important stages in the struggle of the industrialization of Brazil (1914-64), minimal institutional, political, and cultural conditions were created for the consolidation of a decidedly urban-industrial civilization. In these years, especially after 1945, the masses began to participate in political decisions and in the formulation of aims for national progress. As a consequence, two more models for development were organized. From the conflicts between the various economic groups and social classes during the fifty-year period emerged four basic models for the development and organization of the Brazilian economy.

1) The oldest and at the same time the most conservative was the export model. This model implied the hegemony of the agricultural sector, which followed traditional processes of production and techniques of savings. It had its necessary counterpart in the importation of manufactured goods and involved an external dependence owing to the international commercialization of the principal crop, coffee. Moreover, the decision-making centers that were most important for the formulation and execution of economic policy in Brazil were

located overseas. In the period when this model of organization of the national economy was predominant, political power was exercised by the agrarian, commercial bourgeoisie, whose strongest and most organized nuclei were situated in the states of São Paulo and Minas Gerais. The groups interested in this economic policy and the power structure associated with it suffered a serious defeat with the success of the Revolution of 1930, but their defeat was not total.

2) Following this model and arising from its inadequacy in attending to the fast-growing needs of the economy and the national society, the model of substitution of imports was constituted. It formed a positive and dynamic union with the agrarian sector, linking the requirements of foreign exchange credits with the requirements of investments destined for the internal market. This model involved the reformulation of foreign ties with the traditional society. Based on the rule of the masses and state control, the model of substitution of imports established gradations in the structural breaks that were indispensable for its execution. It was built on an independent foreign policy and implied in its doctrine that Brazil be an autonomous power. The basic elements of this politico-economic pattern were transformed into the populist democracy that arose after 1945, forming the nationalist model.

3) In concomitance with, and as a consequence of, the confrontation between the export model and the substitution model there was set up the economic development model in which national and foreign, political and military capital and interests were associated. This model implied an increasing internationalization of the industrial sector along with a fundamentally international character in the traditional agrarian

sector. To a certain measure the international model, or that of full association, is one of the inevitable results of the confrontation between, and the contradictions arising out of, the two previous models. In a certain sense it is a restoration of the initial model, the colonial one, but under new conditions. We are dealing here with a product of international and national economic and political developments. In the conflict of interests of the economic groups and social classes struggling for power and for the formulation of economic policy, there necessarily arose a compromise model of development. For it to take hold necessitated the elimination of populist democracy as a national political structure, as well as the destruction of the doctrine of political and economic independence. The result was a new alliance between the agrarian and industrial sectors in the field of expanded growth of capital. This model will be examined in its most important aspects in the third part of this work.

4) The fourth model for national development was socialist. It resulted from the conflicts and antagonisms between the economic groups and social classes. To a certain degree this model was constituted in concomitance with the substitution model. Sometimes they actually have been confused or tacitly associated. This error in identification arises from the fact that both really were possible negations of the other two, although in various degrees. Involved was the rejection of the traditional model of exportation and the model of international association. Frequently state intervention, the efforts of economic planning, the practices of the rule of the masses, reforms, and vigorous cultural and political growth were considered as prerequisites or even conquests of a socialist type.

THE NATIONALIST EPOCH

This is the setting at once theoretical and historical in which we must study the rule of the masses as a fundamental component of the nationalist model of economic development. As industrialization progressed, especially in the stage from 1945 to 1961, the rule of the masses was a crucial element. Let us see how it was characterized.

The union of economic and political interests of the proletariat, the middle class, and the industrial bourgeoisie was an important element of *getulismo*. This effective and tactical alliance of interests was designed to favor the creation and expansion of the industrial as well as the tertiary sector (commerce). In addition, democratic institutions were created designed to guarantee that the workers would have access to a portion of power. Actually getulismo created a struggle for a greater sharing in productivity. On a broader level it was an alliance of forces destined to strengthen the rupture with traditional society and predominant foreign sectors at an accelerated pace. In reality getulismo was based on developmental nationalism as the ideological nucleus of the rule of the masses, in which were involved civilian and soldier, liberal and leftist, worker and university student, and which saw the return to Brazil of some decision-making centers that were important for the formulation and execution of economic policy. The growing participation of the federal government in the economy was at the same time a necessity and a consequence of this program of nationalizing decisions.

In this context belong the victories of the salaried working classes, especially the proletariat. In 1940 the system of the minimum salary was set up. From 1943 on the Labor Laws appear as the most important instrument for the interchange of interests between the salaried workers and the entrepreneurs.

In 1963 the Rural Worker's Statute became a law and a new element in the development of the rule of the masses.

The interchange between the classes was executed with efficacy, in a good part at least owing to the spoils system — a practice inherent in the structure of labor legislation. It kept the labor unions and the middle class dependent on the Ministry of Labor (initially the Ministry of Labor, Industry, and Commerce; later simply the Ministry of Labor) through the management of financial resources. The union tax, an amount equal to one day's salary, created by the administration and deposited to and supervised by the Ministry of Labor, was a source of revenue for the union.[1] Here lies one of the most important elements of the spoils system. The union directors are elected in general on the basis of agreement and supervision of the Ministry, that is, the government. Under these circumstances the unions and their directors are reduced to instruments of political maneuvering, occasionally contrary to the interests of the workers. Or again, the workers and business leaders are obligated to formulate a line of political action congruent with governmental interests in some form. As we can see, the formalization of labor relations under the terms of the Labor Laws and the Rural Worker's Statute delineates and limits the political action of the working classes.

A further element that is important in understanding the political structure of the rule of the masses is the rural-urban composition of the industrial proletariat. This is one of the factors for the political naïveté of the Brazilian people. With the internal migration to the cities and industrial centers, particularly intense after 1945, the relative contingent of workers without any political tradition was augmented rapidly. Their cultural horizon was marked profoundly by values and patterns of rural life. Patrimonial or communal forms in the organization of power, leadership, and submission predominated. In particular the social and cultural universe of the farm worker has been traditionally bound by mysticism, violence, and conformism. This cultural horizon was modified in the city and in industry but in a slow, partial, and contradictory manner.

In the relations of the worker to the factory, the foreman, the manager, etc., there persisted active elements of a communal type which placed itself between people and things. For this reason the definition of "they" is not political according to the connotation of the relations between the seller and the buyer of labor.[2]

In the first years of his integration into the urban-industrial environment, although this was a period of simultaneous social mobility, the understanding that the worker held of other social types was ambiguous. For a rather long time the more important stages in the process of resocialization evolved. In order to convey an idea of the importance and the scope of these conditions of existence for the worker in the urban and industrial nuclei, it is well to look at the data in Table 6 relative to urbanization. They can be considered at least indicative of the trends that we are examining.

The processes of urbanization and industrialization are not unique causes for the migratory movement to the cities. Despite the fact that they were the most important reasons for the exodus, parallel to them were modifications operating in the rural environment. Little by little capitalistic technology in the rural areas expanded, producing unemployment and the expulsion of a portion of the labor force.

TABLE 6

RATES OF URBANIZATION

	1940	1950	1960
Brazil	31.2	36.2	45.1
Geographic and economic regions			
North	27.8	31.5	37.8
Northeast	23.4	26.4	34.2
Central West	21.5	24.4	35.0
Southeast	39.4	47.5	57.3
South	27.7	29.5	37.6
Regions of Law No. 2,973			
Developed	37.1	43.5	52.5
Underdeveloped	23.5	26.5	34.5
São Paulo	44.1	52.6	62.8

Source: Data from the Division of Regional Studies of the Economic Department of BNDE.
Note: Regions: I. Developed: including the Southeast and the South excluding the state of Espírito Santo. II. Underdeveloped: comprising Espírito Santo, the North, the Central West, and the Northeast. These categories are based on criteria for the activities of BNDE according to the definition found in article 34 of Law No. 2,973 of November 26, 1956. Cf. Luiz Carlos de Andrade, "Desenvolvimento Regional — Problemas e Perspectivas," *Revista do BNDE*, I, No. 2 (Rio de Janeiro, 1964), 87-116. Data were taken from p. 101. The states which make up each of these specified regions will be found in Table 7.

In addition, the rapid increase in the means of communication, including that due to the movement of groups and individuals, results in a comparison of the material conditions of existence. Various possibilities open to workers in the country and the city are contrasted. In other words, an effective demonstration also arises as an important element in the movement of people. In consequence, the bright lights of the city assume a fundamental importance in the characterization of the conditions and nature of the rule of the masses. The data presented in Table 7 give a clear idea of the discrepancies in income which influenced, and which continue to influence, decisions and expectations in general.

For all these reasons a singular conscience prevailed among the urban and industrial proletariat. The proletariat's heterogeneous composition and recent formation, when associated with the exigencies of the rule of the masses led by other social groups, favored the creation and persistence of a conscience for social mobility. That is, it favored the formation of individual or group behavior principally centered upon conquest and a consolidation of positions in the social scale. During this period the political activity of the proletariat as a collective unit was more strongly organized in terms of a mass conscience. Class interests and, in particular, antagonisms with other economic groups and social classes were only partially organized. The proletariat had not come to build upon positions and political directives that were authentically proletarian as a class.

More than this, the rule of the masses in Brazil was directed essentially toward development. The reported redistribution of wealth under getulismo was unreal, since the cost of living always absorbed all of the effective salary, and generally more. Furthermore, a type of forfeiting of wages was evident prior to getulismo. The data in Table 8 clearly reveal this.

The regime of the minimum salary began in 1940, and united with the victories of the Labor Laws put in effect in 1943, had the object, among others, of keeping the working class from drastic impoverishment. At the same time it was designed to keep the processes of production in line with the requirements of economic development. It is well to observe

TABLE 7

PER CAPITA INCOME IN RURAL AND URBAN AREAS, 1960

(Current rate in cruzeiros)

States and Territories	Total	Urban	Rural
BRAZIL	27,005	40,178	16,194
North	16,261	30,033	7,900
Amazonas	24,898	47,968	13,417
Pará	15,704	28,582	6,878
Northeast	13,564	21,413	9,477
Maranhão	9,214	23,056	6,169
Piauí	7,710	17,903	4,566
Ceará	12,038	19,405	8,292
Rio Grande do Norte	15,177	18,457	13,206
Paraíba	14,430	15,123	14,056
Pernambuco	16,194	23,158	10,522
Alagoas	13,526	18,797	10,852
Sergipe	14,653	21,493	10,297
Bahia	14,913	24,382	9,861
West Central	15,896	17,363	15,105
Goiás	14,715	17,240	13,607
Mato Grosso	20,909	21,860	20,288
Southeast	37,631	50,405	20,467
Espírito Santo	17,285	27,784	12,345
Minas Gerais	18,991	24,801	14,095
Rio de Janeiro	25,446	29,333	19,363
Guanabara	77,963	79,014	37,908
São Paulo	47,600	58,005	30,024
South	29,771	39,288	24,026
Paraná	29,651	34,864	27,304
Santa Catarina	23,997	36,748	17,897
Rio Grande do Sul	31,137	42,412	23,766
Regions of Law No. 2,973			
Developed	35,975	48,529	22,126
Underdeveloped	14,195	22,070	10,039

Source: Department of Economics, BNDE. Raw data from Getúlio Vargas Foundation, Brazilian Institute of Reinsurance.
Note: The figures on income refer to weighted internal income comprising rural and urban income, income from the agricultural and non-agricultural sectors respectively. Cf. Luiz Carlos de Andrade, "Desenvolvimento Regional — Problemas e Perspectivas," *Revista do BNDE*, I, No. 2 (Rio de Janeiro, 1964), 89.

that the labor legislation legally and politically formalizing the relations of the working classes among themselves and with the entrepreneurs and public authority was ratified during the Estado Nôvo of the Vargas regime. However, this legislation did not prevent the level of actual wages from continuing to remain below the indices for the cost of living.

TABLE 8

INDICES OF THE COST OF LIVING, WAGES, AND INDUSTRIAL PRODUCTION

			Industrial Production		
Year	Cost of Living	Wages	Brazil	São Paulo	Other Regions
1914	100	100	100	100	100
1915	108	100	118	119	116
1916	116	101	140	145	139
1917	128	107	197	206	193
1918	144	117	171	181	167
1919	148	123	209	226	202
1920	163	146	188	206	180
1921	167	158	188	208	179
1922	184	163	218	244	206
1923	202	181	303	345	285
1924	236	211	194	224	181
1925	252	233	178	208	165
1926	260	236	193	228	178
1927	267	240	217	259	199
1928	263	253	284	343	257
1929	261	251	269	328	242
1930	237	240	260	322	232
1931	228	235	265	332	235
1932	229	275	253	329	219
1933	227	270	273	350	239
1934	245	276	289	376	251
1935	256	283	343	451	296
1936	291	283	345	459	296
1937	312	300	375	503	319
1938	318	315	394	534	331

Source: Roberto C. Simonsen, *A Evolução Industrial do Brasil* (São Paulo, 1939).

In this manner there continued to be a forfeiture of wages and consequently a progressive increase of return on capital. This is what we discover in Table 9, which gives continuity to the trends revealed by the data in Table 8.

Owing partly to the rule of the masses, it was possible to accomplish determined stages of industrial development. By means of juridical and political techniques inherent in getulismo, the relation between the cost of living and the effective wage was maintained on a level proportionate to industrial progress. In a larger sense it was populist democracy that reconciled interests in the name of nationalistic development in order to benefit industrialization. Thus in Brazil getulismo furnished the political and ideological bases for the realization of indices of savings adequate to maintain levels of investment necessary to speed up industrialization. In particular, inflation as a technique for disguised and forced monetary savings was benefited fully by the manner in which the

TABLE 9

REAL MINIMUM SALARY IN RIO DE JANEIRO
(Base 1952: 100 = Cr$ 1,200)

Year	Cost of Living	Nominal Minimum Salary in Cr$	Real Minimum Salary in Cr$	Per Capita Gross Product
1952	100	100	100	100
1954	146	200	137	104.8
1956	226	316	142	107.4
1959	367	500	136	120.2
1960	644	800	121	124.2
1961	867	1220	129	129.8
1963	1454	1750	120	

Source: *Desenvolvimento e Conjuntura*, February, 1962 and January, 1964. Cf. Centro de Desenvolvimento Econômico CEPAL-BNDE, *15 Anos de Política Econômica no Brasil* (Rio de Janeiro, 1964), p. 120.

processes of production were formalized in the urban-industrial milieu.

To sum up, the rule of the masses worked as a technique
for the organization, supervision, and utilization of the political power of the working classes, particularly the proletariat.
On one side was the need for savings to finance investments
that would develop the secondary sector. On the other was
the revolution in the expectations of workers. These two
trends joined in provoking and effecting successive redefini-
tions of the relations of urban-industrial segments with the
traditional segments and the external sectors.

In this context appears the problem of ties between popular
movements and political parties in Brazil. Before 1930 political parties were state-oriented or only nominally national,
and they were concerned with the interests of the oligarchies
and regional social groups. Even after the Constitution of
1946 set up the system of national political parties, the parties
generally continued to follow local and regional interests. In
many cases the oligarchies continued their predominance but
restated their promises and created new techniques for action.
An examination of the coalitions between parties that occurred
in the various elections after 1945 reveals the multiplicity
of possible combinations. The various platforms were never
insurmountable obstacles. Parties came to be defined as "right"
or "left" depending upon their region of the state or country
and independent of their definition on a national level. According to an analysis by Orlando M. Carvalho:

> The division of the electorate into parties with the same social
> composition facilitated a growing number of alliances and coali-
> tions in the parlimentary elections. In 1945 there were no coali-

tions; in 1950 they reached 20 percent of the electorate; in 1954 they attracted 33 percent of the votes.[3]

In 1954 in Pernambuco the following parties formed a co-alition: the Social Democratic Party (PSD), the Christian Democrat Party (PDC), the Social Progressive Party (PSP), the Liberator Party (PL), and the Popular Representation Party (PRP), which united organizations from the center and the right according to their national definition. In the 1958 elections, on the other hand, a coalition of parties of the same state of Pernambuco united the National Democratic Union (UDN), the Brazilian Labor Party (PTB), the Social Progressive Party (PSP), the National Labor Party (PTN), and the Brazilian Socialist Party (PSB), thereby placing side by side organizations from the right, the center, and the left.

This situation disturbed the politicians interested in exercising a more effective leadership on the national level. Yet their preoccupations and condemnations did not upset the customary methods of the leaders and partisan organizations of the various states and regions. Getúlio Vargas and Jânio Quadros were absorbed with this problem and attempted to transform it into a matter for the executive as well as the legislative. In their own words:

We are forced to recognize that bossism and rural politics have not yet been definitely surmounted. Time is needed in order to eradicate deep-rooted vices. On the other hand, as a substitute for cliques it is necessary that leaders appear with ideas that capture the understanding and confidence of the masses. Indispensable for a completely free electorate is freedom from fear and want, which can be achieved by a substantial elevation in the standard of living of the most numerous segment of our people. My constant pre-occupation has been the achievement of a social and economic democracy by means of the protection of the laborer and the improvement of living conditions for the poor.[4]

Whatever is said regarding political representation, the basilar part of the democratic system, there is a general cry for systematic law for political parties and, consequently, reform of electoral legislation. One must strengthen the political parties, ensuring them a greater voice in the life of the nation and reciprocally imposing upon them greater responsibilities, not merely in the episodic periods of elections, but permanently, disciplining them in party conventions; ensuring them an independent financial life but supervising their expenses so they do not become bound to economic groups nor altered by the abuse of propaganda or the influence from vested interests — the authenticity of popular manifestation.[5]

Formal platforms, mass movements, and charismatic leaders stimulate the people. It is conceivable also that the platforms only make sense to them when they are identified with an individual — a leader; in general, the president; at times, the governor; and more rarely, the deputy, the mayor, or the councilman.

Actually the rule of the masses is an unfolding of the political events that led to a partial rupture between urban-industrial society and traditional society, together with external political and economic systems. For this reason it has reappeared many times in the recent past as a technique for the formulation of foreign affairs. Developmental nationalism was at the heart of the petroleum campaign of 1947 to 1953. An independent foreign policy is a manifestation related to the type of populist democracy found in Brazil.

In a certain sense there was a doctrine of extortion underlying the manner in which the nationalist model for economic development was put into practice in Brazil. That is, it played off the interests of one nation against those of another, seeking to gain the best political and economic conditions in the defense of a nationalistic economic policy. For example, the Vargas government succeeded in installing the steel mills at Volta Redonda (begun in 1943) owing to a skillful playing off of the United States against Germany. While the United States desired the adherence of Brazil against the Axis Powers, Germany sought Brazil's neutrality. Actually it was the United States that financed the enterprise and furnished the initial technical assistance. According to some interpretations, this was to have been the price for the alignment of Brazil with the United States and the Allies. Moreover, some documents taken from the Germans and published by the U.S. State Department reveal that the factory was on the agenda for German-Brazilian discussions in 1943. According to a message of the German ambassador to Brazil, Kurt Max Pruffer:

The trip of a Brazilian envoy to the United States continues to be very uncertain here. They say, nevertheless, that the United States has offered very favorable financial conditions.

Inasmuch as the negotiations are evidently an operation that forms part of the intense economic offensive that America is waging against Germany, I request authorization by telegram to relate the following to the Brazilian government or to the President: (1) We are prepared to purchase Brazilian products, especially coffee and cotton, immediately after the war. In addition, if necessary, we are prepared to sign the purchase contracts right away; and (2) we are ready and in a position to fulfill the contract for the steel mill within a normal period of delivery and to agree to accept in principle Brazilian products in payment.

These communications will be destined at the same time to strengthen the political position of the Federal Council in face of the present attempts of the Americans and the Allies to undermine it.[6]

Afterwards, during his second presidential period (1951-

54) Getúlio Vargas continued to be preoccupied with the extent to which a program for national economic development needs to take into account international economic and political systems. With each step there is the problem of keeping or strengthening the external ruptures. According to Vargas in 1951:

Brazil faces intensive economic development with an imperative that cannot be postponed and that is in perfect harmony with other American countries.

This development does not depend only on internal financial and economic policy that is to be authorized by the government. Worldwide economic conditions are more important than national. The success or failure of any policy depends in the first place upon its perfect dovetailing with regional and world tendencies, which in a large part determines the consequences of the actions of the various governments.[7]

Tensions were aggravated with the expounding of the rule of the masses and the program for industrialization, as well as with the creation of new institutional bases for independent economic development. In 1953 Vargas signed a law which created a state enterprise for oil exploration, Petrobrás. Following this the political crisis worsened. The conflict between the various projects for economic development and the organization of power became crucial. In 1954 the antagonism between those who supported internationalized development (or association with foreign organizations) and those who wanted to expedite independent economic development became complete. It was a period in which the depth of the ruptures with external sectors and traditional society was to prove itself if a new stage in the nationalist model was desired. Vargas' suicide demonstrates the victory of those who wanted to reformulate and strengthen relations with international capitalism. In many respects, the suicide statement of Getúlio Vargas is a synthesis of the getulismo spirit as it concerned his relations with the masses, his economic policy, and his relations with leading nations. In addition, Vargas' death and the document indicate the apex of the civilizing processes of populist democracy.

Once again forces and interests against the people unite and strike out against me. They do not fight me openly, they slander me and do not give me the right to defend myself. They must drown my voice and impede my actions, so that I no longer continue to defend, as I always have defended, the people, and especially the humble poor.

I follow the destiny that is imposed upon me. After decades of domination and plunder by international financial and economic groups, I led a revolution and I won. I initiated the job of liberation and I established a regime of social liberty. I had to resign. I returned to the head of the government on the arms of the people.

The underground campaign of international groups became allied to national groups that had revolted against the rule of guaranteed work. The law against excess profits was detained in Congress. Wrath was unleashed against the justice of a revision of the minimum salary. I wanted to create national liberty in increasing the potential of our natural riches with the founding of Petrobrás. This began badly because of the wave of agitation which enveloped it. Eletrobrás was hindered until the point of desperation. They do not want the worker to be free. They do not want the people to be independent.

I assumed the government in the middle of an inflationary spiral that destroyed the value of labor. The profits of foreign companies reached 500 percent yearly. In the declarations of imported articles there were verified frauds of more than $100 million a year. The crisis in coffee came, increasing the value of our principal product. We attempted to defend its price and the response was a violent pressure upon our economy to the point where we were obligated to surrender.

I have fought hour after hour, day after day, month after month, resisting the constant, incessant pressures, supporting everything in silence, forgetting all, renouncing it only to myself, to defend the people who now, unsupported, will fall. Nothing more can I give you if not my blood. If the vultures want someone's blood, if they want to suck the Brazilian people, I offer my life for the holocaust. I choose this way to remain always with you. When they humiliate you, you will feel my spirit suffering at your side. When hunger beats at your door, you will feel in your heart the energy to struggle for yourself and your children. When they scorn you, you will feel in my thoughts the energy for reaction. My sacrifice will keep you united and my name will be your battle flag. Every drop of my blood will be an immortal call in your conscience and will maintain the sacred heartbeat for resistance. To hatred I answer with pardon. And to those who think they have defeated me, I answer with victory. I was the slave of the people and today I liberate myself for eternal life. But this people whose slave I was will no longer be the slave of anyone. My sacrifice will remain always in their hearts and my blood will be the price for their redemption.

I fought against the pillaging of Brazil. I fought against the pillaging of the people. I have fought with an open heart. Hate, infamy, slander did not batter my spirit. I gave my life to you. Now I offer my death. I fear nothing. Calmly I take the first step on the road to eternity and I leave life to enter history.[8]

The administration of Juscelino Kubitschek was a singular demonstration of the political and economic components implicated in the crisis that destroyed the Vargas government. Since it was not possible to establish a dictatorship to finish off populist democracy at one stroke, Kubitschek's government was forced to make conciliations: it maintained and supported the rule of the masses but accomplished a program for economic development based upon the internationalization of new investments. Paradoxically, while there was talk about the "denationalization" of Brazilian industry, new economic organizations sought to combine with foreign capital. The Kubitschek administration allied the Vargas scheme of political support (including nationalistic economic development) with an economic policy that was a return to internationalization, but structured differently. Furthermore, the populist government of Jânio Quadros and the labor government of João Goulart only showed one side of the coin. The other side was defective, since they had neither the conditions nor the ability to restore the nationalist model in its entirety, although great efforts were made in this direction. The *Plano Trienal* which was to have been put into execution between 1963 and 1965 was an attempt to recapture the economic dimensions of the nationalist model of development. The doctrine of an independent foreign policy was a daring experiment in this direction. We are able to observe this attempt in the writings of Jânio Quadros, San Tiago Dantas, and João Goulart.

Without damage to our rate of economic growth our balance of payments does not permit us to dispense with the contribution of foreign capital in the form of investments or financing, while it can collaborate effectively to intensify the economic dynamics of the country under the guarantees that our laws concede to private enterprises. But such a contribution will be subordinated to the fundamental interests of Brazilian development and national security. The entry of this capital will be selective, encouraging that in sectors where we consider cooperation convenient or advisable at our present stage of economic development and discouraging that where the advantages do not compensate for the burden. Furthermore, it will not be admitted without a simultaneous guarantee to Brazilian enterprises of effective competition by modifying the laws and regulations which place the Brazilian company in an inferior position. And the same imperative for the subordination of competition from foreign capital in the national economy as a whole will call for urgent restrictions on all those profit remittances sent abroad that are immoderate or that constitute an intolerable flight of funds.[9]

Leaving aside the previous evolution, let us say that the international orientation of our country, which depends upon our position in the face of concrete questions, has evolved constantly toward an attitude of independence in relation to the politico-military blocs. This cannot be confused with other attitudes commonly designated as neutralism or a third position and which do not dissociate us from democratic and Christian principles upon which our policies have been molded.

This independent position allows us to search for the line of conduct most in keeping with the objectives that we envision before each problem or international question without having had a previous compact with any bloc of nations or obligation for joint action, excluding, of course, the regional obligations related in the OAS charter and the Rio de Janeiro Treaty, and also without the systematic exclusion of any others whatsoever in the formation of different policies or ideologies.[10]

In the economic position of Latin American countries in international associations it becomes necessary to exercise a vigilance to prevent negative effects from being sensed in a serious manner whether it be in the balance of payments, or in the unrestricted flow of profits and dividends, or in the preferential directing of capital toward the extraction of raw materials and the exportation of agricultural products. It is indispensable that the expansion plans of large private enterprises be adjusted to the essential priorities of development, objectively identified. . . .

The foreign policy of the government has obeyed an inalterable principle regarding the sovereignty of other peoples as the guardian of our own independence. It has been a long time since Brazil has been able to think itself free from the responsibilities of major international questions. Today we are one of the most populous democratic nations and our legal and political traditions confer authority for us to carry on constructive action in a debate of the great problems of the modern world, seeking always to contribute with the best of our ability toward the preservation and the strengthening of peace.[11]

CHAPTER 6

RULE OF THE MASSES IN THE RURAL ZONES

The antagonisms between the city and the country were based initially on conflicts between the model of agriculture for exportation and the model of industrialization for the internal market. Entrepreneurs and capitalists struggled with this point on various levels. On one side they fought for the retention of the economic surplus and on the other for the maintenance or modification of the economic structure. This struggle manifested itself directly and indirectly in the realm of political power. The coups and revolutions in Brazil after 1922 were related to this confrontation in various forms.

After that time an ever-increasing portion of entrepreneurs, following the conventions of capital and its applications, joined and interlocked one with the other. Economic groups, simple and complex, national or associated with foreign companies, were formed. Thus the processes for the concentration and centralization of capital on national and international levels entered into ever more complex stages involving agriculture and industry. For this reason controversies were weakened or acquired different connotations.

Following this phase, new kinds of antagonisms arose from the heart of the agrarian society itself. The large landowners and the workers began to clash. Let us first characterize these two categories, ignoring the small and medium-sized agricultural establishments.

The large landowners are entrepreneurs, ranchers, plantation owners, or latifundists. Their properties can be divided into two principal and extreme types, the agricultural enterprise and the latifundium. The first is an actual capitalistic enterprise such as the sugar mill, the coffee plantation, or the sugar or cocoa plantation. The second is not classified as an enterprise. It is an agricultural establishment consisting in the organization of various factors with traditional labor relations. It is a large unit divided into autonomous subunits organized according to subsistence productive activities and partially commercialized. However, whether an agricultural establishment is classified as an enterprise or a latifundium depends upon the degree of effective utilization of the factors of production, especially the labor force. Other establishments possess the actual labor force and occasionally some agricultural machinery.

It is obvious that the worker's place in the productive process is fundamental for the classification of the economic undertaking in the rural milieu. Moreover, one should not confuse the social definition of the laborer with the significance of his work and, consequently, the product of his activity. Depending upon what his labor achieves (in the market for its commercial value or in the community for its usefulness), the laborer will or will not be an element of an enterprise or a latifundium. A greater or lesser exploitation is not sufficient to define the precapitalistic or capitalistic character of the undertaking. To the contrary, it can be useful in classifying the degree of economic surplus as income and profit. We should understand the concept of agricultural workers regardless of the local or regional social classification such as settler, sharecropper, migrant worker, contractor, renter, tenant farmer, hired farmhand, peon, or rubber-gatherer.

TABLE 10

ACTIVE ECONOMIC POPULATION IN 1950
According to Principal Activities

(*in percent*)

Country	Primary Activities	Secondary Activities	Tertiary Activities
GROUP A	73.5	11.1	15.4
Haiti	83.2	5.6	11.2
Honduras	83.6	6.9	9.5
Guatemala	68.4	14.3	17.3
Nicaragua	68.7	14.2	17.1
Salvador	63.4	14.4	22.2
GROUP B	58.9	16.2	24.9
Brazil	60.3	13.5	26.2
Mexico	59.0	14.7	26.3
Bolivia	74.8	12.9	22.3
Dominican Republic	56.5	9.5	34.0
Costa Rica	54.9	15.9	29.2
Colombia	55.5	16.1	28.4
Paraguay	53.9	18.7	27.4
Ecuador	53.6	21.7	24.7
GROUP C	34.2	24.3	41.6
Panama	49.9	9.8	40.7
Cuba	42.0	20.3	37.7
Venezuela	43.9	15.7	40.2
Chile	34.8	24.7	40.5
Argentina	25.7	27.8	46.5
GROUP D	17.0	33.2	49.8
Canada	21.0	33.5	45.5
United States	13.1	32.9	54.0

Source: United Nations. Cf. "La Situación Demográfica en América Latina." *Boletín Económico de América Latina*, VI, No. 2 (Santiago de Chile, October, 1961), 47.

THE NATIONALIST EPOCH

TABLE 11

COMPOSITION OF AGRICULTURAL LABOR, 1950

Workers a	* 1	2	3	4	5	6	7
Total	6,017,297	4,077,383	67.8	1,098,642	18.3	840,272	13.9
Tenant farmers	466,615	258,379	55.4	115,413	24.8	92,823	19.8
Squatters	575,881	284,257	49.3	164,710	28.6	126,914	22.1
Employees	3,729,244	2,734,154	73.3	582,483	15.6	412,607	11.1
Permanent	1,420,867	993,953	69.9	218,674	15.4	208,240	14.7
Temporary	2,308,377	1,740,201	75.4	363,809	15.7	204,367	8.9
Sharecroppers	1,245,557	800,593	65.0	236,036	18.9	208,928	16.1

Source: Serviço Nacional de Recenseamento. Cf. *Conjuntura Econômica*, Ano X, No. 12 (Rio de Janeiro, December, 1956), p. 75.

ª Workers on land not owned by them.

* Column 1 — Total; 2 — No. of Men; 3 — Percent of Men; 4 — No. of Women; 5 — Percent of Women; 6 — No. of Children; 7 — Percent of Children.

In order to convey an idea of the relative importance of the agrarian society as a part of the system which includes the urban-industrial society, let us examine in Table 10 the distribution of the active population according to the primary, secondary, and tertiary sectors of the national economy. The contrast with fully industrialized nations will be useful to heighten the relative importance of the primary activities. The specific importance of the agrarian civilization is seen better as a system generated from colonial stages of the nations concerned.

It can be seen that the comparison between Latin American countries and the United States and Canada shows a relative and absolute weighting in the agrarian sectors above others. Thus not only the character of the productive process in Brazil becomes clear, but also the predominance of the agrarian over the urban-industrial society.

In relation to Brazil the data acquire greater significance

when considered in detail in Table 11. It is necessary to observe the composition of the labor force on lands not owned by the worker in order to have an idea not only of the structuring of the labor force but also of the mobility of groups and individuals within the strata of agricultural workers. In this case one sees the meaningful presence of the woman and the child as important parts of the labor force in the rural world.

The composition of men, women, and children in the labor force, or permanent and temporary workers, is important in characterizing conditions for rural-urban migrations. On the one hand, it becomes easy to find a substitute for the man going to the city or to factories. On the other hand, the departure of the man (which is the rule) more than the woman or child relieves social tensions, decreasing the conflicts about work and labor claims, since these usually originate from the more experienced males. Sometimes the migrants are men of action or men with potential qualities for leadership and organization. They have a broader cultural horizon than the average, and the migration of these persons to the urban centers represents a loss of vanguard elements. This, however, is only one aspect of the question.

Considering the level of the present population, we see that the total number of individuals in the agrarian society has diminished. Owing to the attraction of living conditions in the cities and industrial centers or because of technological and organizational innovations in process in the country, the relative population employed in primary activities shrinks little by little. In a parallel fashion the relative population in the secondary and tertiary sectors is augmented. Figures showing this situation are presented in Table 12.

In general, however, conditions of retardation, extreme

TABLE 12

POPULATION ACCORDING TO OCCUPATION

(10 years and older)

Occupation	Population			Percent		
	1940	*1950*	*1960*	*1940*	*1950*	*1960*
Agriculture, cattle raising, forestry	9,453,512	9,886,934	11,697,798	32.56	27.04	23.99
Mining	390,560	482,972	573,443	1.34	1.32	1.18
Manufacturing	1,137,356	1,608,309	2,069,962	3.92	4.40	4.25
Construction	262,700	584,644	785,014	.90	1.60	1.61
Commerce	749,143	958,509	1,520,046	2.58	2.62	3.12
Transportation, communications, and storage	500,184	697,089	1,088,798	1.72	1.91	2.23
Service activities	1,437,320	1,672,802	2,732,148	4.95	4.58	5.60
Others	827,823	1,226,103	2,184,054	2.85	3.35	4.48
Inactive	14,279,251	19,440,628	26,110,204	49.18	53.18	53.54
Total	29,037,849	36,557,990	48,761,467	100.00	100.00	100.00

Source: Serviço Nacional de Recenseamento. Cf. Instituto Brasileiro de Geografia e Estatístico, *Anuário Estatístico do Brasil* (Rio de Janeiro, IBGE, 1965), p. 35.

poverty, and exploitation do not directly nourish political tensions in the agrarian world. The conflicts inherent in the processes of production in the rural society only acquire a political character when they are the very components of a class situation. Even though the social and cultural universe is predominantly impregnated with patrimonial and communal values and patterns, the workers cannot formulate their claims in purely political terms. In an existence marked by communal and traditional patrimonial patterns we see that coerced votes, village politics, *coronelismo*, highwaymen, banditry, mysticism, the *mutirão*, and *compadre* relations are the chief ways of life for both the landowner and the worker.

Social tensions intertwine with mysticism or with individualized violence and anarchy. The worker does not employ cultural and intellectual expedients to define the landowner or the overseer as "they." Everyone participates equally as "us." When the worker thinks of the overseer or the landowner as "they," he is not considering them as part of a political category but only as part of a social category established by tradition, luck, and family ties.

It is only when the conditions of production are modified that labor relations lose communal and patrimonial overtones and acquire political ones. This process can be witnessed in Porecatu, Paraná, and in Santa Fé do Sul, state of São Paulo, as well as in the humid zone of Pernambuco. In Santa Fé do Sul in 1960 social tensions acquired political overtones when farm workers felt they were on the verge of being converted (with the termination of the contract signed with the landowners) into workers without work or workers looking for work. To a certain extent they began to understand their position in the market situation as virtual sellers of labor, which in fact they were. They did not see any possibility of renewing the contract on the basis under which they had been living until then. Thus began legal disputes and their inevitable political result — armed conflict.

By means of a contract valid for one year or one harvest the sharecroppers faced the following problems at the end of the agreement:

Besides those referred to under other items the sharecroppers will have under this contract the following rights and obligations:
a) he has the right to construct in the area allocated a house for his occupancy and any improvements necessary for the execution of this contract, but at the end of the contractual period he will

not have the right to indemnity nor retention of what he has done, being able, however, to remove the roof tiles and the barbed wire that he has employed;

 b) he has the right to construct a well or cistern contiguous to his house but he is obligated to fill it up or cover it at the end of the present contract;

 c) work animals: the sharecropper may keep or pasture in a fenced area in the allocated land such animals necessary to work his fields. He may not leave animals loose or any part of the farm since the farm does not provide pasture lands for the said animals.

 d) the sharecropper must leave the necessary right of way at the boundary of his fields with that of his neighbor for the free circulation of workers, employees of the landowner, and vehicles necessary for the farm.

. . . .

 12. The sharecropper, in the period from December of this year to the end of January of next year, must plant grass (*capim colonião*) in the area given to him. This should be done observing the maximum distance of 16 *palmas* between rows and pits, being in the minimum four seedlings in each pit.

 13. The cessation and total or partial subleasing of the rights of this contract are permitted only with the express approval of the first contractant.

 14. Terminating the present contract by the expiration of its term or by its cancellation in the form stated in the law, the sharecropper must give up the house without prior notification or challenge. A just motive for cancellation, besides the provisions in the law, is the violation of the obligations stated herein.

 15. If the sharecropper discharges the terms of the present contract to the letter and leaves the farm at its termination, the debts he had with the first contractant and those originating from the previous contract and renewed here will be pardoned, these debts being taken care of by the grass planting and the produce of the agricultural year just terminated.[1]

Because of the character of the contract (a leonine partnership in its effects, particularly in terminating itself) the renters initiated legal revindications. Little by little the conflict acquired political overtones. According to an article published in a daily newspaper on the very day during which the relations between the landowners and renters worsened:

> Contrary to alarmist rumors disclosed in the capital of the state [São Paulo] — all pointing toward electioneering and social and political agitation — there is order in the *município* of Santa Fé do Sul. The population is calm and the situation is tranquil in the city and its districts of Rubineia, Três Fronteiras, Santa Clara, and Santana do Ponte Pensa, very different from last year. There is no fighting between the landowners ("latifundists") and the exploited "peasants," to employ communist jargon. Everything centers on the discontent of about 50 families of direct and indirect renters, of the rancher José de Carvalho Diniz whose contracts already have expired or are about to, and who against the desire of the landlord intend to remain on the rented land, alleging automatic renewal of the contract by force of the tenancy law. Of these 50, some have not fulfilled the expired contract, infringing upon its clauses; others executed it, but are found to be incompatible with the landlord.[2]

These are some of the more important points in the proletarianization of the agricultural workers and in the transformation favoring the appearance of legal and political factors in tensions with the landowners. In a sense the proletarianization of the farm worker is in progress, or, even better, a new stage is going on in the transformation of the tenant worker into a salaried worker. The problem the new contingent of laborers in various categories face is in selling their labor. This proletarianization becomes more real in the views of the people themselves, whether it be in the urban-industrial scene or in the transformation of the farm into an actual enterprise. The introduction of political thinking to the rural workers occurs the moment the relations of production change to a capitalistic type. In this instant the communal and patri-monial values and patterns no longer enjoy the conditions necessary to sustain themselves or at least to allow them to predominate. The worker acquires the basic outlook for the definition of the landowner or the overseer as "they," not only as someone belonging to another family group and pos-sessed of a prominent fortune and traditions, but as the politi-cal "they."

Celso Furtado has described perfectly the manner in which proletarianization is seen in the humid zone of the Northeast. He follows the fundamental aspects of the process in an ex-tremely clear interpretation.

The industrialization of the country, bringing with it an increase in per capita income and intense urbanization, has provoked an appreciable increment in the consumption of sugar in the course of the present decade. As a matter of fact, from less than 30 million bags in 1953-54 the local consumption exceeded 46 million in 1962-63. On the other hand, extremely favorable conditions in the world market allowed full recovery of exportations, which gave rise to a growth in production even more intense than that in consumption. The Northeast participated in this new prosperity, raising production in the last decade around 50 percent. However, it happens that this augmentation in production was made in the customary manner of simple incorporation of new lands into cane fields, lands that are almost always inferior to those previously under cultivation. Since average yields per hectare cultivated remained stationary around 40 tons, it can be inferred that the methods of some few landowners in introducing irrigation systems and in the use of fertilizer were just sufficient to compensate for the incorporation of lands inferior in quality. This being the case, it can also be deduced that there was an elevation in the average production costs and a diminishing yield during the recent period of expansion granting constant relative prices for raw material and product.

RULE OF THE MASSES IN THE RURAL ZONES

The increase in production that we have considered has led to two types of practical consequences; first, the pressure to extend the cane fields brought the progressive elimination of areas previously given over to food production; second, the tendency to elevate real costs created a strong pressure on the workers' salaries.

The extension of the areas under cane cultivation had consequences of profound social and economic significance. In a relatively short period the squatter was transformed from a very small farmer, responsible for the production of that which he and his family ate, into a simple salaried worker. From his restriction in an isolated shack on top of a hill where his family lived without being conscious of neighbors, he was pushed to the edge of the highway where he could not plant even a handful of earth. It was necessary to give a substantial monetary salary increase to this worker for him to feed himself by buying the food he formerly was producing. In this manner the transformation of the squatter into a simple salaried worker carried with it an elevation in the cost of labor without any corresponding augmentation whatsoever in productivity. The squatter was a semiseasonal worker who reverted partially to a nonmonetary economy of subsistence during the period when the demand for labor was low; this made him an extremely cheap kind of labor, since the land that he used for his subsistence farm had no alternative economic use. As soon as there arose a need for this land the same worker required a much higher salary in order to survive. The pressure in the direction of elevated workers' salaries arose concomitantly with the pressure already referred to from the elevation of real costs of production, originating from the incorporation of lands poor in quality.[3]

These profound economic and social changes were accompanied by the appearance of various political leaders on the rural scene. Outstanding among the new leaders in the Northeast are Francisco Julião, federal deputy of the Brazilian Socialist Party and organizer and leader of the first Peasant Leagues; Miguel Arraes, mayor of Recife and later governor of Pernambuco (1963-64) when his mandate was removed, and a member of the Brazilian Labor Party (PTB); Celso Furtado, economist without party affiliation, organizer of SUDENE, whose program consisted of energizing the productive forces and modernizing the agricultural and industrial enterprises throughout the arid Northeast; Padre Melo of the Catholic Church, who was connected with the Brazilian Institute for Democratic Action (IBAD), an organ that worked openly against Arraes and Julião. In addition to these leaders, more important in the decade from 1955 to 1964 were groups and leaders linked with the PTB, with the Catholic Church (as the Popular Action Party, AP), and with the Brazilian Communist Party.

Because of his position as governor of a key state in the Northeast (Pernambuco) and his political position in labor, Miguel Arraes held an important role in the region. He can be considered as one of the most typical representatives of leftist getulismo. In a sense it was Celso Furtado with SUDENE and Miguel Arraes with the labor party who brought the Revolution of 1930 to the Northeast. As governor, Arraes acted to formalize and modernize labor relations favoring the democratization of political power. In this he was directly and unquestionably following the rule of the masses of the nationalist model for economic development. Let us look at some of his major thoughts.

Upon taking away from the police the traditional function of guaranteeing the secular privileges of a minority, while simultaneously creating conditions for the free exercise by all of the democratic rights assured by the Constitution, the government attained in its first year of office one of its fundamental goals. Arising from a concept of order and liberty that deviated from the customary tendency of considering them as conflicting, this was the first conquest won and, certainly, the most important.

This new conception of state political power alongside rapid organization of the rural working masses permitted a profound social transformation in the Pernambucan sugar-cane zone.

The conditions that were prevalent there for a long time assumed a character that was frankly incompatable with the requirements for the development of Pernambuco and the country. Surviving artificially because of a protectionist policy and federal government subsidies, sugar-cane production perpetuated wholly outdated methods. In agriculture principally, the backwardness assumed alarming aspects, being translated into yields per hectare that were the lowest in the world. There was no incentive for new investments; to the contrary, the sugar policy of the federal government administered through the Sugar and Alcohol Institute encouraged stagnation as an obvious loss for the nation and the state.

Besides the myopic protectionist policy of the Sugar and Alcohol Institute, one other mechanism contributed considerably to ensure the sugar industry a precarious yield: the maintenance of extremely low salary levels, a poor price for daily labor, is exhausting for the majority of rural workers.

It is true that emergence of numerous and powerful rights movements became inevitable, given the state of misery and oppression in which the workers of the sugar-cane zone lived. Thanks, however, to the mobilization of all the state apparatus for the intransigent defense of a privileged unprogressive minority, the process of organizing the workers of the rural zones was suffocated and almost disarticulated in the vain attempt to block the advance of already obvious social forces on the political scene.

It is clear that this situation could not last, based as it was on the misery of the working masses, who little by little became cognizant of themselves and their problems. This slow process of self-awareness, truly relentless in its internal dynamics, and manifesting itself in a sporadic and disorderly manner, presented itself

79

to the eyes of the privileged minority as supreme subversion. History is full of similar examples. Abolition of slavery in 1888 was not considered any less subversive.

With the emergence of favorable conditions created by the government, the process of organization and, consequently, the political maturation of the workers in the cities and in the country made considerable and rapid progress in Pernambuco. This is particularly true in the cane zone of the state.

Congressional approval of labor legislation for the rural zones created favorable legal conditions for the rupture of relations of a semifeudal type still prevalent in whole sectors of our agricultural economy. This legislation, however, considering that it resulted from a political movement with a base more in the cities than in the country, tended inevitably to be unenforced, following the example of other legal guarantees, since conditions for its immediate implementation were not created. In Pernambuco it was possible to unite the two most favorable conditions: a growing rural labor movement with a degree of consciousness and organization, and a truly democratic government capable of assuring its free manifestation in the defense of rights and legitimate claims.

To the organized and democratic movement of cane workers in their legitimate aspiration for an improved standard of living belongs the indisputable merit of ventilating the suffocating climate in which the cane industry lived. A pressure from below generated by a broad stratum of rural workers, who no longer would tolerate the conditions under which they lived, was necessary in order to arrive at the tardy discovery that sugar cane cost money to produce. And this occurred because an expressive few, who were part of that price and who up until then had remained invisible, manifested their existence in a decisive and clear manner.[4]

As we can see, the orientation of Miguel Arraes toward the workers repeated in the Northeast what the Revolution of 1930 had made possible in the principal regions of the South Central States. In other words, the rule of the masses and getulismo came to the Northeast and to the rural zones after a delay of many decades.

In this historical context the Peasant Leagues were created and later rural labor unions. However, the leagues and the unions were not able to bring radical political action quickly. Francisco Julião, who symbolized the leftist radical leader in the rural Brazilian milieu, and especially in the Northeast, knew that the agricultural workers who were organized into leagues, associations, and unions did not have the political experience to advance the revolution. He knew that the scythe in the worker's hands was still an instrument for lawless violence, not revolutionary violence. The mind of the worker overcome with his own situation did not permit him to distinguish clearly between the league and the union, the union boss and the leader, the priest and mysticism, Julião and Jango (João Goulart). For this reason, with the Rural Worker's Statute (Law No. 4,214 of March 2, 1963) the Peasant Leagues began to be replaced quickly by rural labor unions. Or, in other words, the organizations and leaders of the Catholic Church or the Communist Party or the Labor Party substituted Francisco Julião in the region or progressively reduced his power.

In 1962 Padre Melo tried to calm the more conservative sectors:

Padre Melo states that the phenomenon of Peasant Leagues tends to extinguish itself gradually. These entities, being civil societies, only shelter those whose participation interests them, and this causes them to lose force in face of the movement for organizing rural unions which every day grows in the Northeast. Moreover, he denies that the leagues at present or at any time had a communistic character or were the work of only one individual [an allusion to Francisco Julião].

The Padre explained the absence of communism in the leagues by the profound ignorance of the peasants, which allows them neither to have any principles nor to organize themselves around their necessities.[5]

Thus the rule of the masses that developed in the urban-industrial milieu expanded and gained vigor in the rural zones. The unions were founded with the same spirit as the industrial workers' unions. That is, their assistance and recreational character overrode their political character. In 1954 the Agricultural Workers' Union of Brazil (ULTAB) already had been founded in São Paulo and on January 1, 1955, the first peasant league, the Agricultural and Cattle-raising Society of Planters of Pernambuco, was created. In December, 1963, the National Confederation of Agricultural Workers (CONTAG) was founded. Table 13 shows the number of rural unions in existence in December, 1963.

In summary, the form in which the agricultural proletariat engaged in national politics was similar to that practiced by the industrial workers' unions. Under certain aspects the entry of rural workers into the political struggle inspired by class consciousness occurred according to the techniques of the rule of the masses formulated in the urban centers. Moreover, even Miguel Arraes recognized that labor legislation for the rural society "resulted from a political movement with a base more in the cities than in the country." In this sense populist democracy overflowed into the rural zones and alarmed the agrarian bourgeoisie. Outstanding among the most daring claims of the agricultural proletariat were the right to unions and political organization, and agrarian reform. The struggles formed around these goals facilitated the growing mobilization of the peasant masses. In a large part the First National Congress of

TABLE 13

RURAL UNIONIZATION IN BRAZIL

(as of December 31, 1963)

States	Recognized Unions	Unions Awaiting Recognition	Recognized Federations	Federations Awaiting Recognition
North		6		1
Rondônia				
Acre				
Amazonas		1		
Rio Branco				
Pará		5		
Amapá				
Northeast	92	193	4	17
Maranhão	3	14		1
Piauí	2	16		3
Ceará	21	22	1	2
Rio Grande do Norte	19	41	1	4
Pernambuco	32	58	1	4
Paraíba	11	20	1	1
Alagoas	4	22		2
East	24	123	2	7
Sergipe	9	9	1	
Bahia	2	19		2
Minas Gerais		57		4
Espírito Santo		11		1
Rio de Janeiro	13	23	1	
Guanabara		5		
South	143	211	3	8
São Paulo	61	60	2	1
Paraná	47	71	1	3
Santa Catarina	2	5		1
Rio Grande do Sul	33	75		3
West Central	11	24	1	
Mato Grosso	1	3		
Goiás	10	19	1	
Federal District (Brasília)		2		
Total	270	557	10	33

Source: Superintendência Para a Reforma Agraria. Cf. Robert E. Price, "Rural Unionization in Brazil" (1964), MS, p. 83.

Laborers and Agricultural Workers that met in Belo Horizonte in November, 1961, concentrated on these proposals:

With the goal of realizing agrarian reform that truly interests the people and the rural working masses, we judge it urgent and indispensable to provide solutions to the following questions:

a) Radical transformation of the existing agrarian structure with the elimination of a majority of land ownership by the latifundists, principally by expropriation of the large estates by the federal government, substituting for the monopolistic proprietorship peasant ownership in individual or partner form and state property.

b) Maximum access to the possession and use of the land by those who wish to work it, based on sale, usufruct, or rent at moderate rates of the land expropriated from the latifundists and the free distribution of unoccupied land.

In addition to these measures which envision a radical modification of the existing bases of the agrarian question, solutions such as the following are necessary to improve the present conditions of living and work of the peasant masses:

a) Respect for the broad, free, and democratic right of independent organization of the peasants in their class associations.

b) Effective application of labor legislation already in existence, which is extended to the agricultural workers, as well as immediate government preparations to impede its violation. Development of the "Statute" that endorses adequate labor legislation for the rural workers.

c) Full guarantee for free and autonomous organization of unions for the salaried and partially salaried workers in the country. Immediate recognition of rural unions.

d) Effective and immediate assistance for the peasant economy of all types.[6]

This declaration unites typical elements of leftist reformism compromised by the rule of the masses. Here we find associated fundamental themes of agrarian society and the characteristic language of the popular left. In other words, once more the agrarian society and the urban-industrial society are combined in the rule of the masses.

CHAPTER 7

THE LEFT AND THE MASSES

The Brazilian Left understood that the cyclical ruptures initiated by World War I and developed as a result of the 1929 Depression and World War II had profound repercussions on the internal structures of Brazilian society. Leftists saw the relation between international conflicts and internal struggles that produced such results as the communist revolution in Russia, China, and Cuba as well as independence in India, Egypt, and Algeria. The Left realized that the coups, revolts, and revolutions that occurred in Brazil after 1922 were internal manifestations of crises in the capitalistic colonial system.

However, this same Left was unable to deepen the political ruptures in Brazil in order to lead the country to socialism. Its comprehension of the situation never reached the point of profoundly winning over the urban proletariat, to say nothing of the agricultural proletariat (as well as such middle-class sectors as intellectuals and students), to the stage of inciting a revolution. This is the general dilemma that faced the Brazilian Left during the remarkable struggle to surmount the colonial economy and to win cultural, political, and economic emancipation.

Confronted with conflicting political conceptions of various economic groups and social classes, the Left sought to formulate and define an alternative policy of its own. In the face of the models presented and adopted by different sectors of the dominant class (export, substitution, and international), the Left had to create its conception of socialist progress. It looked to theoretical and practical traditions of Marxism-Leninism for a revolutionary solution. However, it needed to adjust to local conditions. As the principal stratagem, a reform policy was developed that was amply supported by the policy of substitution of imported items. This orientation prevailed after 1945.

Before this date, however, the Left was committed to diverse forms without organizing its own project in a convincing manner. It fluctuated between theoretical Marxism-Leninism and *tenentismo* as an effective political route, and between revolutionary theory and putschism, which was put into practice in the uprising of 1935. In addition, it was compelled to develop a persistent and frequently difficult struggle against *integralismo*, the dictatorship of the Estado Nòvo, and Nazism, and for the granting of amnesty for political prisoners, among them Luiz Carlos Prestes and Agildo Barata who were confined during the entire period of the Estado Nòvo from 1937 to 1945. From its foundation by a group of workers and intellectuals in 1922 until the end of World War II, the Communist Party prepared partisan and auxiliary cadres and gained experience in its effort to mold a theory of revolution for a society that was entering the industrial epoch. The dilemma lay in discovering a practical correspondence for the theoretically formulated contradictions.

After 1945 reform predominated with an internal political orientation. On the international level the first project was opposition to North American imperialism, whose support in Brazil is thought to come from the latifundists. Therefore the fight for basic reforms was considered the most effective route to attack simultaneously the interests of the latifundists, commercial bourgeois sectors, and imperialists. In order to advance this campaign the Communist Party favored establishing alliances with the workers, middle-class sectors, university students, intellectuals, populist politicians, the military, and, principally, sectors of the bourgeoisie. The leftist interpretation of nationalist development inferred that the interests of significant sectors of the industrial bourgeoisie in the internal market were brought into opposition with the latifundists, the importer, and imperialists. Thus a *united front* between the Left and the bourgeoisie could lead the struggle for economic progress, growing democratization, and working-class victories.

To be more precise, the Left tacitly adopted the model of substitution of imports as a necessary step in the Brazilian revolutionary process. Moreover, this tacit position led to the adoption and involvement of the rule of the masses, which became one of the main elements of populist democracy. Whereupon the second serious dilemma arose for the Brazilian Left: it could not transform the rule of the masses into the revolt of the classes.

Actually the Brazilian Left only occasionally shunned the direction and initiative established by the vanguard of the dominant class. On the one hand, the political struggles were related to institutional reforms organized and led by the industrial bourgeoisie with the support of the middle classes. Tenentismo and, later, nationalism transformed these struggles ideologically. They were concerned with redefining foreign relations and those with the traditional society for the purpose of urban-industrial expansion. This project was oriented around acceleration of the transition from an export policy to a policy of substitution of imports. At the same time it became urgent to heed some of the requirements for the democratization and social mobility of the middle-class groups, both civil and military. Besides this, the formalization of labor relations in the budding industrial sector and in the tertiary sector was imperative. The coup of November 10, 1937, ushering in the Estado Nòvo was destined fundamentally to control growing social unrest. Moreover, the reformulation of foreign relations and those with the traditional society continued. The governing apparatus underwent important changes that brought it up to present-day needs in some sectors. With the creation of the Steel Company of Volta Redonda and the Labor Laws (1943) the first practical results of structural significance were witnessed from the reform movement begun two decades previously. Following this came the National Economic Development Bank (BNDE), Petrobrás, SUDENE, etc., as developments of the same general process of institutional changes and renovation of the productive forces of the secondary and tertiary sectors.

On the other hand, the initiatives and directions established in the most dynamic sectors of the industrial bourgeoisie took form in the rule of the masses. After assuming the presidency of the Republic through the Revolution of 1930, Getúlio Vargas gradually but completely transformed the relations of public authority with salaried workers, especially skilled workers.

The Labor Laws were not the only important element in the structure and development of the rule of the masses. Let us see how this ideology was depicted in the evolution of the political thought of Vargas, Kubitschek, and Goulart.

1931: Apropos, it is well to observe that lately unjustifiable suspicion of the collaboration of organized unions, which were created under the stimulus of common necessity and class interests, has become apparent.

The new laws recognizing these organizations principally had in mind their legal aspect, so that instead of causing a negative force hostile to public authority, they should become socially a profitable element of cooperation with the governing mechanism of the state. Thus is explained the advisability of dividing up the body politic, each group having its own characteristics similar to those of political parties, each being represented according to its own electoral strength.

1938: The state neither wants nor recognizes class struggle. The labor laws are laws for social harmony.

1940: Political discipline must be based on social justice supporting labor and the laborer so that he is not considered a negative value, an outcast from public life, hostile or indifferent to the society in which he lives. Only in this manner can a cohesive national nucelus be constituted, capable of resisting disorder and the seeds of disintegration.

It is necessary that the proletariat participate in all public activities as an indispensable element for social collaboration. The order created by new situations that leads nations is incompatible with individualism, at least when it is in opposition to collective interest. It does not allow any rights that transcend obligations to the fatherland.

1940: It has always been my desire to solve the problems of the relations of labor versus capital, to unite, harmonize, and strengthen all the elements of these two powerful forces of social progress. I act thus not only in obedience to the principles of political order but also guided by sentiment, by the conviction that only in peace and brotherly understanding can men achieve their aspirations for material and cultural perfection.

1940: Class prejudice, as it is conceived and discussed by extreme reformers, never preoccupied us in the organizing of social laws. In a society where individual interests prevail over collective interests, the revolt of the classes can arise as a reaction with tragic consequences. For this reason, social laws in order to be satisfactory and adaptable must express a balance of the collective interests, eliminating antagonisms, adjusting economic factors, transforming the worker finally into a common denominator for all useful activities. Labor is, therefore, one's first social duty. The worker as well as the industrialist, the employer as well as the employee, truly are devoted to their duties and are not differentiated in constructive energy in the eyes of the nation; they are all laborers. Before them and against them there is only one class in permanent antagonism whose harmfulness must be combated and reduced to a minimum—that of the men who do not contribute to the enrichment of the country, the idlers and the parasites.[1]

1947: It is the duty of the workers to guarantee their own future, inserting themselves as a majority into the political circles of the country and fighting for progress and the union of the Brazilian family.

The Brazilian Labor Party is the political weapon of the proletariat. We are certain that the fight we are joined in today will not be in vain because the decisive inspiration for the present revolution is found already in the spirit of our people, in shaping the system of social equality.

In the future the Brazilian people will no longer be divided between rich and poor, powerful and humble. They will be one people united by understanding, by a sense of a commonly shared happiness.

The first of May should be then the date for the brotherhood of all classes, exalting their collective strength.[2]

1960: To maintain social peace, together with an improvement in the worker's standard of living and a parallel increase in production, was the object of constant support by the government every time its interference was necessary in salary demands.

Thanks to the understanding between employees and employers, settlements were reached quickly with adequate solutions even when strikes were about to erupt. These were of short duration and did not produce notable shocks in the economic structure or in social harmony. . . .

The administration was interested in the greater reconcilement of the workers and at the same time sought to remedy institutions destined for their protection by keeping idle elements away.

The government sees with gratitude that local and national professional organizations are multiplying and in the majority of cases have at their heads directors whose intellectual level shows the high index of political awareness in the Brazilian working and employer classes. The courses in union formation and in the publicizing of labor legislation advanced by various organs of public authority and by private bodies contributed in a large part to the development of these groups that today are cooperating with the public authorities in some administrative sectors.[3]

1963: Labor problems, the principal factor in production and national wealth, have been gaining special attention from my government. To ensure adequate laws and to fight for their enforcement, to advance resolutely a salary policy that improves the buying power of the worker, to provide him with a strong union organization as the guarantor of efficient collective labor contracts, has been, is, and will always be basic goals of the social policy of my government.

Despite misunderstandings in some sectors, I have undergone constant effort to give the workers and their families, which means the Brazilian people in general, a standard of living that is more human and more dignified, which is their incontestable right. Much still remains to be done. But a considerable part that was needed already has been accomplished. In the course of the year 1962 various laws promulgated by me corresponded to the specific claims of the labor classes. . . .

The recent promulgation of the Estatuto do Trabalhador Rural, product of laborious study and debate in Congress, is one of the most important landmarks in our labor history. Without being ignorant of the practical difficulties to be surpassed in its execution, I am certain that it will form a very powerful instrument for economic and social redemption of the rural individual and one of the fundamental conditioners for an effective agrarian reform. Rural unionization, a basic factor in the implantation of true and unified social progress in the country, has become a steady pre-occupation of my government. Only by this can the rural workers organize in a disciplined and systematic fashion for the protection of their interests. A good union organization is essential to the very outcome of such new labor legislation as the recently published statute.[4]

1964: The responsibility in the historic mission of making Brazil economically independent cannot and should not fall exclusively on the laboring classes, who are exactly the ones who carry out a considerable role, who are precisely the weakest economic groups, and who cannot dispense with the support and the protection to which the state must remain alert.

This among other things is one of the principal functions of labor legislation and social welfare, whose best application and constant perfectioning will depend directly upon the results of our policy for economic development.

Moreover, better comprehension of the rights and duties in employment relations, their respect and observance; more efficient help in sickness, invalidism, old age; the certainty of a decent standard of living; social-medical assistance; reeducation and professional readaptation to provide the workers and their families with the security and the indispensable tranquillity of fruitful and constructive labor, all this is the mainspring of any public or private enterprise and an essential part of any economic development program.[5]

Thus the Labor Laws, the Brazilian Labor Party, union bossism, the Rural Worker's Statute, Vargas, Kubitschek,

THE NATIONALIST EPOCH

Goulart, Arraes, and Brizolla [6] form part of a continuous system. Alongside them we can place Ademar de Barros, former mayor and governor of São Paulo, Hugo Borghi, Jânio Quadros, and others as parts of the same populist universe. All these men are related to the Vargas way of thinking and particularly to the rule of the masses as a nuclei-linked element or variant thereof. The rule of the masses is one of the basic features of populist democracy.

In this historic and ideological context the Brazilian Left was imprisoned. The techniques of the rule of the masses and reform led by the most resolute of those advocating industrialization established the limits and conditions for political awareness, as well as for political activity of the urban proletariat, of certain sectors of the middle class, of university students, and afterwards of the agricultural proletariat. As a consequence, the Left oscillated between Marxist recommendations and the requirements of populist democracy. It was not capable of converting the rule of the masses into the revolt of the classes. It neither formulated nor implanted an alternative interpretation that corresponded with the structural historical possibilities, nor did it succumb to the fascination of the nationalist ideology.[7]

However, the evolution of the rule of the masses was not peaceful. To the contrary, concessions in rural and industrial labor legislation, for example, were the result of actual claims arising from repeated tensions and conflicts that accumulated in the collective experience. As the national economy developed and diversified, especially with industrialization, strikes multiplied. In the interplay among the entrepreneurs, the salaried workers, and the political organizations, tensions became aggravated and led to impasses. The frequency of strikes indicates the strength of the proletariat and the salaried workers in general in defending the buying power of their salary. Often the leftist organizations and leaders organized and led the strikes.

Tables 14, 15, and 16 show the character of class relations in the industrial society. The large number of strikes, and of strikers and industries involved in them, is indicative of the manner in which the workers resisted the deflating of their actual salary. Among the alleged motives for the outbreak and maintenance of strike movements, economic reasons are uppermost. In addition, among the professional sectors the participation of the textile workers, the most archaic sector in Brazilian industry, is outstanding. The strikes were rarely centered around political reasons; however, frequently communists, socialists, *petebistas*, and other leaders sought to give them a broader political connotation. All strikes acquired a political significance to some degree depending upon their emergence and the direct and indirect effects on the union environment, on the working class, and on other sectors of society. On this level those leaders and organizations mentioned above repeatedly exercised an active and resolute role.

Generally, although the union directors always sought to intervene to a greater degree in the broader political problems of the country, it was obvious that they did not have the conditions for massive mobilization of the class as a pressure instrument for the attainment of the proposed objectives.[8]

The workers' participation in strikes motivated by economic questions is not great. In quantitative terms it can be said that they participate much more by omission than by deliberate and persistent action. In this regard one can observe that even the number of unionized workers is small. If the union still

95

TABLE 14

STRIKES IN BRAZIL IN 1951 AND 1952

Year	Number of Strikes	Number of Strikers	Number of Enterprises Affected
1951	173	363,999	548
1952	264	410,890	922

Source: Jover Telles, *O Movimento Sindical no Brasil* (Rio de Janeiro, Editorial Vitória, 1962), p. 57.

TABLE 15

STRIKES IN SÃO PAULO IN 1961 AND 1962

Year	Number of Strikes	Number of Strikers	Number of Enterprises Affected	Number of Man-Hours Lost
1961	180	254,215	954	3,252,062
1962	154	158,891	980	3,067,474

Source: *Revista de Estudos Sócio-Econômicos* (São Paulo, Departamento Intersindical de Estatística e Estudos Sócio-Econômicos, January, 1962), p. 23.

has not gained the confidence of the workers and has not awakened their interest, then it is obvious that their capacity in relating to and accepting the union leaders is minimized. This is a consequence of the actual structure of the Brazilian working class, whose formation was rapid and recent, whose origin was rural, and whose composition is influenced by new age and sex groups. This fact is basic for an understanding of the rule of the masses and the limits and conditions for action imposed upon the Left.

Even strikes bearing a deliberate political stamp, such as the general strike of July 5, 1962, are not free from immediate and explicit economic objectives. At least such objectives are an

THE LEFT AND THE MASSES

TABLE 16

Motivation	Number of Strikes	Percent
Salary increase	96	36.3
Payment of back salary	38	14.4
Sympathy	27	10.2
Improvement of working conditions	13	4.9
Payment of Christmas bonus	9	3.4
Warnings	7	2.6
Against shortages	7	2.6
Against government ceiling for the minimum salary	3	1.1
Various strikes (lack of information)	64	24.2
Total	264	100.0

Source: Jover Telles, *O Movimento Sindical no Brasil* (Rio de Janeiro, Editorial Vitória, 1962), p. 58.

important ingredient to stimulate the interest of and mobilize the working-class sectors. The aims of the general strike were formulated by the union heads of the following organizations: National Stevedores' Federation, National Maritime Workers' Federation, National Railway Workers' Federation, National Longshoremen's Federation, National Typesetters' Federation, National Warehousemen's Federation, United Longshoremen of Brazil, and the Permanent Commission for Union Organizations of Guanabara.

The complaints that united the different professional groups for action were the following:

1. Effective fight against inflation and product shortages, mobilizing all means of transportation for the carrying of essential foodstuffs from productive centers to consumers, even confiscating existing supplies, if necessary;

2. Radical and immediate agrarian reform, with recognition of the rural workers' unions;

97

3. Urban reform as the only solution for the individual home-ownership problem;

4. Bank reform with the nationalization of deposits;

5. Electoral reform giving illiterates and corporals and soldiers of the armed forces the right to vote, and the institution of a single ballot for the October 7 elections.

6. University reform and the participation of one third of the students in the assemblies and departmental and university councils;

7. Expansion of the present foreign policy of Brazil through establishment of new markets, defense of peace, total disarmament, and self-determination for the people;

8. Repudiation and exposure of the financial policy of the International Monetary Fund;

9. Approval of the law which guarantees the right to strike, within the terms of the project approved by the Federal Chamber of Deputies with the proposed amendments and previously approved by the workers in their meetings;

10. Expropriation with inventory of all foreign enterprises exploiting public utilities;

11. Control of the entry of foreign capital into the country and restriction of remittance of profits;

12. Workers' participation in profits;

13. Revocation of all and any agreements injurious to national interests;

14. Strengthening of Petrobrás with a state monopoly for the importation of crude oil, for the distribution of derivatives, for the petrochemical industry and the expropriation of private refineries;

15. Effective measures for the functioning of Eletrobrás;

16. Creation of Aerobrás, thereby instituting a state monopoly in commercial aviation;

17. Maintenance of the present autonomies in sea transportation, ensuring that 50 percent of all imports and exports will be carried on national merchant vessels;

18. Approval of the law instituting the payment of the thirteenth-month salary.[9]

United here in a single platform are the current political objectives of the rule of the masses and those specifically of the Left. In the formulation of these claims the Left needed to conform to the reformist requirements inherent in the workings of a populist democracy. It grasped the situation and defined its program with the uncertainties of the struggle in mind. In the end, however, the Left did not escape from the ambiguities of the game, and reverted frequently to the means and ends of getulismo. Studying and delineating the plans and the duties of the Communists in the union movement, the Left established the following principles:

The principal and never-ending task of the Communist movement consists in uniting and organizing the working class, increasing its awareness, and directing its fight, so that it can fulfill a leading function in Brazilian society. The working class will play an ever more important role in the political life of the country to the degree in which it strengthens union harmony.

The Communists are not the only ones in the union movement nor can they assume an attitude of exclusive partisanship. There are numerous inclinations among the workers, many think differently from the Communists, but all need to unite to strengthen the working class. The Communists think that the unions should not be used for achieving objectives that divide the workers. To the contrary, they must be the instruments for the uniting of workers of all inclinations in the struggle for their rights. With this belief the Communists made a great effort to fulfill the role of solidifying the diverse currents in the union movement and to organize the nonunion workers, who were still a majority. The uniting of Communist-, Labor-, Socialist-, and Catholic-oriented workers, as well as unaffiliated workers, was the principal weapon the working class possessed to fight for its rights.

Union harmony can only be achieved via unity of workers' actions around the common and most strongly felt claims, no matter how basic they be. In order to reach this unity of action it is necessary to utilize the victories of existing social legislation and try to solidify and perfect it, by influencing Parliament through the pressure of the masses. The Communists acted within the boundaries of the union structure and observed the Labor Laws, seeking within the law to organize and unite the workers toward the fight for their economic, social, and political claims.

Unity can be achieved upon a solid base only if the union movement is to count on the active participation of the working masses and not be solely a movement at the summit. A permanent preoccupation of the Communist should be, moreover, the strengthening of the unions, the realization of unionizing campaigns, as well as the promotion of incentives for inactive union members to return to the union life. Among these incentives the creation of committees is outstanding for the study and protection of the varied interests of the workers, as well as for social welfare, hygiene, job security, salary based on job classification, family allowances, and an adjustable wage scale tied to the cost of living. Similar committees could be formed to deal with the fight against shortages, for the democratization of governmental organs controlling prices, for the cost of living, as well as for interests in sports, recreation, and culture, and for organizing women and children. In order to attract women to the union life, sewing and cooking classes could be initiated. The courses of SENAI and SENAC destined to elevate the professional level of the worker are useful. The classes organized by the Labor Ministry, by SESI, and by other institutions for the purpose of making the Labor Laws known and teaching the workers to read and write should be taken advantage of, fighting at the same time against their negative aspect as preaching "social peace." [10]

This interpretation of the circumstances of the political struggle in the heart of the proletariat is continued with an interpretation of the struggle within the national society. Thus, the leftists define the principal and secondary, the internal and external antagonisms by the strategic and tactical targets in leftist political activity. Among the contradictions, nationalist economic development versus imperialism is conspicuous, as well as the mobility of the peasantry versus the latifundists, involving as tactical objectives the following: basic reforms, a united front with the national bourgeoisie, a worker-student alliance, the stimulation of nationalism and a democratic spirit in the armed forces.

This comprehension of the Brazilian situation was put into practice on different occasions: in the elections of 1945, 1950, 1955, and 1960; in the campaign for amnesty of political prisoners during the Estado Nôvo, and especially on the eve of the liquidation of the Estado Nôvo (1944-45); in the campaign for the states' exploitation of Brazilian oil (1947-53); in the campaign for basic reforms (1961-64); in the campaign for the plebiscite to restore presidential power and prerogatives to President João Goulart (1962-63). On all these occasions the PC, the Brazilian Socialist Party (PSB), large sectors of the Brazilian Labor Party (PTB), and restricted sectors of the Social Democratic Party (PSD), besides unions and union federations, state and national student organizations, intellectual and military groups, participated. The synthesis of this practice appeared in various partisan resolutions, particularly that of the Communist Party.

The Brazilian society is confined by two fundamental contradictions which require radical solutions at the present historical stage of its development. The first is the contradiction between the Brazilian nation and North American imperialism and its agents. The second is the contradiction between the growing productive forces and the land monopoly, which is seen essentially in the struggle between the latifundists and the peasants.

The antagonism between the proletariat and the bourgeoisie inherent in capitalism is also a fundamental contradiction of the Brazilian society. But this contradiction does not necessitate a sweeping and complete solution in the present stage of the revolution since the situation in the country does not present conditions for immediate socialist transformations.

In its present stage the Brazilian revolution is antiimperialistic and antifeudal, national and democratic. These are its essential obligations:

The complete economic and political liberation from a dependence on imperialistic powers, which requires radical measures to eliminate the exploitation of foreign monopolies operating in the country, mainly those of the North Americans.

The radical transformation of the agrarian structure, with the elimination of the monopoly in landownership, of precapitalistic labor relations, and, consequently, of the latifundists as a class.

The independent and progressive development of the national economy by means of industrialization of the country and overcoming the backwardness in agriculture.

The effective elevation of the material and cultural standard of living of the workers, the peasants, and all the common people.

The real guarantee of democratic freedom and the conquest by the masses of new democratic rights.

The realization of these obligations implies the revolutionary transformation of Brazilian society. It demands a profound change in the interrelation of political forces and the passage of state authority into the hands of the anti-imperialistic and antifeudalistic forces, that is, the working class, the peasants, the small bourgeoisie, and the bourgeoisie tied to national interests, among which the proletariat as the most consequential revolutionary force should have the directing role.[11]

This synthesis of the society of the masses, following leftist politics and involving the proletariat, the national bourgeoisie, and other sectors of society, is a combination of the pattern of substitution of imports with basic reforms in the name of nationalistic development. It is the essence of populist democracy as the model for political development. This is the singularity of the Brazilian route to industrialization, economic development in general, and democratization.

Naturally, total adherence to the society of the masses or its tactical adoption was not exclusive with the Communist Party. Other political groups moved in this direction as a recourse to realistic political action. Thus we find side by side the Communist Party (PC), the PSB, the PTB, the Parliamentary Nationalist Front (FPN), the National Liberation Front (FLN), the General Workers' Confederation (CGT), the National Students' Union (UNE), the more radical Chinese sector of the PC, the Workers' Party (POLOP), the Popular Action Party (AP), and the Peasant Leagues led by Francisco Julião. In addition, such leading figures as Leonel Brizolla, Miguel Arraes, Almino Afonso, San Tiago Dantas, and others followed this line, but to the left or right of the formal declarations. There were even movements in which the Clube Militar was engaged, in the name of national defense and economic development.

This is the world of populist democracy in Brazil, striving toward industrialization or seeking an apparently obscure ideal of a powerful Brazil. Some bourgeois sectors appeared to have had the ambition of changing Brazil into a world power in the neutralist bloc. For this reason they accepted the support and the open or veiled collaboration of the Left, depending on the situation. They needed to broaden and deepen the political and economic ruptures with traditional society and foreign sectors. There was a time when the United States under the leadership of John F. Kennedy understood this situation. Instead of drastic action the United States decided to adopt an ingenious orientation favoring modernization and supporting the democratic order. The Punta del Este Charter

(1951) reflects this orientation, which evolved out of Roosevelt's New Deal and Kennedy's New Frontier. This orientation suffered a serious and double defeat, in both Brazil and the United States, with the deposition of João Goulart and the abandonment of "enlightened" imperialism.

On the other hand, the struggle in the heart of populist democracy was considered by the Left as a tactical move for the execution of socialist goals. It was believed that the popular working masses needed to be conquered from the inside according to the objectives and techniques of the rule of the masses itself. For this reason the united front and other obligations with the military and middle-class sectors were indispensable tactical alliances originating from political realism. Thus the Marxist-Leninist theory of revolution was sacrificed momentarily with the object of combining theory and practice, conditions and possibilities, goals and tactics. It is obvious that in this scheme means and ends were confused and inverted. In practice, owing to the vigor, the supremacy, and the realism of the rule of the masses, the Left did not succeed in accomplishing a new and effective revolt of the classes. The political "culture" in populist democracy was more vigorous than the theoretical ability and pertinacity of the leftists.

While it was true that more radical leftist groups existed, they tried to avoid the obstacles or the fascination of the rule of the masses by fighting to preserve ideological purity in theory and practice. The POLOP and the AP each in its own way had this intention. Marxist-Leninist radicalism and Christian radicalism acted to correct the confusion between reformation, opportunism, and revolution. At the same time, however, these groups did not achieve greater successes, not even when exercising the superego functions of the Communist Party.

THE LEFT AND THE MASSES

A document of the POLOP published in 1963 clarifies some important aspects of the dilemma of the Left in Brazil.

1. There are actually in Brazil three revolutionary organizations which, by coordinating their forces, their spheres of activity, and their influence, would be in circumstances to balance the effects of reform and the policy of class collaboration. The latest crisis [referring to the resignation of President Jânio Quadros and the inauguration of João Goulart] demonstrated that they hold a common position. By forming a front, a movement, or whatever one judges necessary, they would be capable of addressing the masses with their very own aspect, initiating a new factor in national politics.

2. The three groups are considered to be Marxist-Leninists and to the degree in which they put their theoretical positions into practice there will be created in the long run a single party representing the interests of the revolutionary proletariat and their allies in the field. The divergences that still persist — and which we do not expect to deny — must be looked upon as part of the process of formation of the party and will be overcome during the course of its own development.

3. We are not proposing the immediate dissolution of the existent organs, which would be abandoning what they already have acquired for something that still has not been determined. Such an attitude will not strengthen the future party and would weaken it, since its formation cannot be a mechanical act but an organic process of growth and development. Only this will assure its survival.

4. Coordination of the activities of the three groups will be the first step toward the creation of a conscious Marxist-Leninist nucleus, in order for a united front of the masses to grow out of the actual struggle. Precisely because such a front will not be Marxist, the existence of an active nucleus will be necessary. Without the Marxist nucleus the front of the masses will not be transformed from an immediate and amorphous agglomeration incapable of resisting its own internal contradictions into the daily politics

of the petit bourgeoisie. This is the secret of the Leninist conception for a vanguard in the struggle of the masses.

5. The task is immediate. The two aspects of the struggle, the formation of the party and the struggle of the actual masses, have to be faced simultaneously. We cannot wait for them to form a party to go out in the streets. There is no "before" and "after" in the dialectics of the struggle of the classes. Without the coordination of the three principal existing groups around definite objectives, there will not be great possibilities of mobilizing decisive sectors of the proletariat. Isolated, not one of the three organizations would be capable of doing this. Without a vital struggle and the mobilization of the masses the existent organs could not overcome their divergences and the much needed party could not be born.[12]

These recommendations were directed particularly to the Brazilian Communist Party (PCB, Russian line), the Communist Party of Brazil (PCdoB, Chinese line), and the Workers' Party itself (POLOP). The internal argument of the Left in general sought to substitute the united front with a leftist front, by freeing the populist, the reformist, and the opportunist Left of mechanical interpretations. In a way this was an attempt to clear the struggles of the Brazilian Left from confusion between ends and means and from the optimism inherent in populist democracy. In this direction the POLOP formulated a rights program pertaining to the cost of living, union freedom and autonomy, peasant struggles, anti-imperialism, and foreign policy. In their general lines, however, the claims presented by this organization were the same as those presented by others, but their formulation was fundamentally more radical. As an example:

Combat speculation in the foodstuffs of the city and the country by confiscating the stock, applying exceptional measures, etc., and eliminating the latifundist; . . .

Dissolution of the Union Fund and the Disciplinary Commission; abolition of the right of intervention, recognition, and dissolution of the unions by the Labor Ministry, as well as of the financial control that the Ministry exercises on the unions via the Bank of Brazil; . . .
Expropriation of the latifundia without indemnification and delivery of the land to the peasants; . . .
Prevention of the remittance of capital, royalties, and interests abroad; . . .
Abrogation of the inter-American treaties and the United States–Brazil Military Agreement.[13]

This attempt at purification of the Brazilian Left found its greatest success with the core of the university youth. It was born with the youth movements. Whether in the name of God or in the name of the devil, the actions of the AP and the POLOP went beyond the university milieu only with difficulty.

Moreover, the students themselves already were engaged in nationalistic and reform movements. Since the end of World War II they had campaigned for amnesty for political prisoners, for national exploitation of oil, for the democratization of political institutions, and for reforms in the teaching system. Later, especially after 1960, they promoted basic reforms, beginning with university reforms, because it was there that the youth placed the problem of the reforms of society. How the university students saw national society from the concrete situation within the university is a "dialectic" argument that was widely diffused. In 1963 appeared the following:

The national political situation, with the growing mobilization of the people, very much favors the movement for university reform, principally if we knew how to bind it to other popular claims. . . .

As a matter of fact, if it is certain that the worker gains political perspective in the majority of cases by his economic claims; if it is certain that the peasant can come to participate more actively in his country's problems by fighting for land, it is not any less certain that the aberrant sphere of higher learning can serve as the instrument for understanding the more general and important questions of our national life. . . .

The alliance with workers, peasants, progressive intellectuals, the democratic military, and other sections of national life must be augmented in the certainty that by uniting our claims we will make them infinitely stronger. This alliance implies that agrarian reform would be the banner of the students in the same manner in which transformations in our teaching system would be the objective and subjective aspiration of the workers and the peasants.[14]

This interpretation by the student organizations in the country was so widespread that the National Students' Union (UNE) sought to synthesize in its program various objectives of university struggles. Thus in the aims of the UNE the following were outstanding:

To secure the solidarity and confraternization of the people based on universal respect for its self-determination;
To influence the government and nationwide public opinion, showing the worth of their purposes;
To increase the Peasant-Worker-Student Alliance.[15]

We can see that the students themselves understood the limits of the "university situation" and the possibilities opened by it. They knew that the specific social and political relations in academic life are also the manifestations of relations in national society. When they attempted to explore this perspective in practical and theoretical terms, they established real and abstract connections between university reform and general transformations in society. According to the analysis of Marialice Mencarini Foracchi:

> Student action only acquired a society-wide view under the condition of its being bound to other social reform forces in Brazilian society. It was only in the degree in which student action was identified with a reform process already going on that it could reclothe itself with a revolutionary connotation.[16]

The rule of the masses functions in the total society as an element of populist democracy. The ruptures desired by the students, as well as those desired by other social groups (including those connected with both the open and the hidden interests of the rural and urban proletariat), are contained in the project for industrialization and total economic development as envisioned in the nationalist model. In this sense the struggles for the transformation of society always are corrected by the techniques and goals of the rule of the masses.

For these reasons the Brazilian Left fluctuated between two poles — Marxism-Leninism and populist democracy. Between the abstract fascination of theory and the effective fascination of practice, the latter always had the upper hand. The political development of the Left in Brazil did not succeed in freeing itself from the development of populist democracy, but was marked by the techniques and ideology of the rule of the masses. If it be true that the vigor of populist politics impeded the Left from winning important victories toward the formulation and implantation of radical ideas, it is also true that on the theoretical level the leftist plans were always unsatisfactory. With the exception of individual expressions, the party platforms never have produced a theoretical formulation sufficient to interpret correctly national and international reality. For this reason the Left never escaped from the fascination of formulas and the jargon of classical Marxism-Leninism. It was a rhetorical fascination as much as the rhetorical fascination of the elite bourgeoisie in relation to the teachings of European and North American thinkers. Thus the Brazilian Left entangled itself in concepts before involving itself in practice. It was concerned obsessively with imperialism, latifundia, the national bourgeoisie, the peasant, the masses, the working classes, basic reforms, and government bureaucracy. In a study on this theme Caio Prado, Jr. points out:

In Brazil, perhaps more than in any other place (since the same evil also existed and still exists in other places), the Marxist theory of revolution, whether direct or indirect, deliberate or inadvertent, inspired all the Brazilian thinking of the Left, and even furnished the general lines for all the fundamental economic reforms proposed in Brazil. The Marxist theory of revolution was developed under the sign of abstractions, that is, of concepts formulated a priori and without adequate consideration of the facts. Later the facts were sought after, and only then, and this is more serious, were they placed within the framework of reality. Or better, an attempt was made to fit the facts to the a priori established concepts. From this a theoretical scheme was derived based in a large part on unreality in which the actual conditions of our economy and the social and political structure frequently appear grossly deformed.

From this resulted the gravest consequence with respect to practice, that is, revolutionary action, since a theory allied in such a manner with reality proved so defective as to make it impossible to extract norms for a consequential policy that could be applicable to concrete situations. As a consequence, the revolutionary policy remained exposed to the whim of immediate circumstances, oscillating continually between sectarian and opportunist extremes without a precise course capable of securely organizing revolutionary action at every moment or in every situation.[17]

THE LEFT AND THE MASSES

In other words, the interpretations that the Left made of the Brazilian social reality (as a whole or in its most significant political and economic moments) were based in general on the unsatisfactory utilization of Marxist dialectics. There was a succession of defeats and frustrations owing to the reversal of ends and means, thoughts and reality. In a formulation of Gramsci:

When one does not have the initiative in the fight and the fight itself ends by identifying itself with a series of defeats, then mechanical determinism transforms itself into a formidable force of moral resistance, coherence, patient and obstinate persverance.[18]

In synthesizing these confusions the Left did not take into account that "masses" and "classes" are not interchangeable expressions. The leftists did not understand that they were dealing with historical and structurally diverse categories. They incurred the semantic illusion proposed by getulismo and its variants. They did not apply themselves to analyzing reality in order to understand that the essence of the popular and working masses is, first, a consciousness of the masses and, second, a consciousness of the classes, and that the principle of social mobility comes before the principle of conflict — that it must follow its own path to, and express, a class consciousness. As long as the Left remained at the level of the consciousness and action of the masses, following in the established patterns of populist democracy, it would remain only a correcting force. For this reason it was always surprised by coups d'état, sudden changes, and lost opportunities. It was that way in 1945 with the deposition of Getúlio Vargas; in 1954 with Vargas' suicide; in 1956-60 in the face of the able combination of the rule of the masses with the major internationalistic development conducted by Juscelino Kubitschek; in 1961 with the resignation of Jânio Quadros and the inciting of the masses by Brizolla; in 1964 before the coup d'état. When confronted with the development of conflicts inherent in populist democracy, the Left did not formulate its own alternatives. Therefore, it condemned itself to impotency when drastic modifications occurred at these important moments in Brazilian history.

CHAPTER 8

CONTRADICTIONS
IN THE NATIONALIST
MODEL

In the various stages of industrialization the Brazilian people accumulated fundamental political experience and developed a new interpretation of their own history. In reviewing their relations with the leading countries of the world and their own national traditions, they gradually formed a new self-image. At times in a disorganized way and on other occasions in a systematic way they examined some of the more important dilemmas and solved parts of them. To a large degree they succeeded in constructing a dynamic vision of the conditions of political, economic, social, and cultural progress. At the same time they redefined the significance of the leadership of the major world powers and the importance of Brazilian traditions. Thus after World War I the enlightening process in Brazil appeared in a unique and creative configuration. From the time of Modern Art Week in São Paulo in 1922 to the founding of the University of Brasília in 1960 there was a succession of artistic, scientific, and political manifestations which clearly expressed this search for new cultural horizons and a new national consciousness.

Intrinisic to this enlightening process was the transformation of social and political spheres of reference. For approximately fifty years the Brazilian people have explored from various angles and generally in a positive way international crises, recessions in coffee production, government control, inflation, nationalism, experiences with economic planning, growing political awareness of the salaried classes, and populist democracy. In this process the Brazilian Left played an important creative role, initiating public debate about problems that other interested political factions had neither the proper orientation nor the courage to express. Independent domestic policy, for example, formulated and put into practice by Vargas, and developed by Jânio Quadros, San Tiago Dantas, and João Goulart, benefited fully from vanguard action and the popular backing guaranteed by the Left. According to an observation of Fernando Pedreira:

> When all is said and done the Left, right or wrong, strong or weak, Marxist or non-Marxist, Catholic or simply liberal, represents the ferment of social and political renovation, the nonconformist impulse of youth and the intellectual elite separated from the establishment.[1]

At the same time getulismo in its full meaning had the ability to attract and absorb politicians and intellectuals from leftist movements. Or it may be that in the field of populist democracy, in the doctrine of the united front, technical and intellectual groups were mobilized for the task of industrialization. It is obvious that in this exchange the decision-making centers were in the domain of the dominant class, that is, those groups who exercised authority directly and indirectly.

On another level, but in the same direction, the bourgeois leaders that were tactically attached to the Left frequently called upon the common people, the masses, the workers, the laboring classes, and the poor. They recognized that the project of national economic development, associated with an independent foreign policy as its inevitable corollary, could not be accomplished without profound internal and external structural ruptures. But they always considered and only admitted partial breaks; thus they were actually reformers. This is the historic and structural background of the following appeals of President João Goulart in 1961 and the Finance Minister, San Tiago Dantas, in 1963.

Truly a people become mature when they come to think for themselves, conditioning their development within the complex of their destiny; this they must forge without xenophobia from familiarity with universal destiny, but also without cowardice of exaggerated mimicry or subservience to the alien. For just this reason Brazil must support the formation of Brazilian teams with Brazilian thinking in order to begin the task of rescuing our country from underdevelopment. Our aim to have a satisfactory operational scheme will not be furthered if we cannot depend on capable men to execute it.

Let us mobilize the people for development in such a way that they are fully conscious of their mission and sense the fruits of the progress that is theirs. Let us build a Brazil that, while keeping the characteristics of its personality and culture, will be new, just, and prosperous. Let us utilize the value of universal suffrage, not as a pseudo-democratic process that furthers artificial representation, but as an instrument of obligation to real, popular causes in a way that permits the people themselves not merely the sensation but the profound conviction that with authentic representatives of their problems it is actually they, themselves, who are governing.[2]

There are nations and epochs in which an enlightened elite frequently promotes and intuitions of the people and succeeds in carrying them to new stages of social development that only later materialize. There are others where the people appear to push society, perhaps without a definite program of action but with an unequivocal sense of renovation. I believe that this is the case in Brazil today and that many of our deceptions and criticisms are resolved by daily proof that on the average the uncertainties and mistakes are harvested from the might of the nation.[3]

Concomitantly with the social, cultural, and political transformations there was a profound economic transformation based on an industrial civilization. Brazilians accumulated experience and technology for the manipulation of the productive forces and institutional conditions in accordance with the requirements of industrial development. Progress was attained to such a degree that some students came to believe that Brazil already had reached or was ready to reach the stage of autonomy. This is what Celso Furtado, Henry Rijken van Olst, and Antonio Dias Leite thought in presenting a new image of national perspectives before 1964.

In attaining a phase of development in which the process of capital formation is supported principally by the internal production of equipment, the development of the Brazilian economy has become the result of her internal dynamics. Therefore, though the external factors still may be more important, the growth rhythm is principally determined by the combinations of decisions made with her own internal market in sight. Furthermore, when the internal production of capital goods reaches a determined degree of development, the maintenance of the level of activity in this sector is only possible if the whole economy continues its growth. In order to avoid large-scale unemployment in the capital goods industries, it becomes indispensible, independent of what occurs in the external sector, to continue an adequate level of investments, which on its side requires motivation for savings compatible only with the high level of productive activity. A reduction in external demand does not necessarily occasion general contraction of economic activity, since it can be compensated by a monetary expansion maintaining the income level and the rate of investments. The inevitable increase in inflationary pressure will be able to affect investment efficiency for a certain period, but the final effect on the rate of growth necessarily will be reduced.

To summarize the observations on the structural modifications that have occurred recently in the Brazilian economy, we see:

a) the conduct of the external sector is no longer the principal factor conditioning the level of economic activity, and the simple maintenance of an elevated level of productive activity engenders an investment volume capable of keeping the economy growing at a reasonably high rate;

b) the process of substitution of imports, necessary for the maintenance of an elevated growth rate in stagnation conditions of the import capacity, requires increased savings per investment unit. The simple continuation of the growth rate implies, therefore a growing inflationary pressure, which in its turn tends to reduce the efficiency of investments and, consequently, the growth rate, even with the hypothesis that the required increased saving is achieved. This tendency can be counterbalanced only by the expansion of import capacity and/or by elevation of investment efficiency through the planning of substitution of imports.[4]

Brazil may be considered at the most advanced country in Latin America. In a short time she will be ready to aid other less developed nations in the Western Hemisphere. Psychologically she is in better circumstances to discharge this role than the European and North American nations, whose motives at times are suspect. Brazil is the natural connecting link between Europe and Africa since she does not possess a past of colonization. All in all, Latin America already follows the actions of Brazil with close attention, since the consequences can have repercussions in many countries of the region.[5]

Since Brazil is not a country that lives by foreign trade, and since it represents only a small part of her total production, she has, in theory, relative freedom to choose the method that is in accordance with the fundamental objectives of her internal economic development.[6]

Populist democracy had before it a unique choice: to continue the Brazilian revolution or to achieve a new stage in the nationalist model. To do this it must strengthen itself by deepening the internal and external structural ruptures. A new phase became urgently necessary for the achievement of its potentialities. Populist democracy proved itself by effecting an independent foreign policy, by expediting the modernization of agrarian society, by engaging new contingents of the Brazilian population in the political process, by encouraging scientific and political discussion about the national scene, by stimulating the flowering of artistic movements inspired by the national society.

Actually the nationalist model never was an over-all project, since it never came to be formulated in a systematic manner. As a political model for development, distinguished by the rule of the masses, it was structured randomly of occurrences, victories, and obstacles. Some groups and leaders perceived its potentialities but they did not succeed in formulating an over-all project. It was a mixture of empiricism and intelligence, courage and strategy. It was the historic result of the actions and interests of different groups and social classes, and was produced in the competition of internal and external antagonisms distinguishing this stage of Brazilian history.

Therefore the nationalist model could be negated only by one of two radical means: socialist revolution or reintegration into world capitalism. Since populist democracy was not capable of formulating a joint interpretation relative to the inherent necessities of its internal dynamics, it fell back upon the alternatives. These alternatives were necessary and inevitable, since they were fixed internally in the nationalist model. They also made up some of the elements that characterized the shape and substance of this model. Since the policy of industrialization was achieved on the basis of conciliations with international capitalism, the traditional Brazilian society, and the urban salaried classes, the socialist model and the internationalist model were always present as possibilities, and became on some occasions more or less feasible. The moment that the actual nationalist model exhausted one stage without continuing into the next, one of the alternatives became imperative. The Coup d'Etat of 1964 was a politico-military operation inherent in the option adopted by the most courageous, and perhaps the most aware, group of the dominant class.

In fact, in the years 1960-64 the Brazilian people were faced continually in a more urgent fashion with the necessity for a drastic option. On the one hand, the nationalist model exhausted a crucial cycle of achievements. A courageous decision was being thrust upon the people to deepen the structural ruptures indispensable to the success of goals inherent in its internal logic. In a definite sense the experiences with the independent foreign policy of Jânio Quadros and San Tiago Dantas, as well as the political exigencies inherent in the Plano Trienal (1963-65), convey an understanding of the dilemma in which the people found themselves. The mobilization of the common people for the mass rally on March 13, 1964, for the purpose of basic reforms and in opposition to the conservative tendencies of the congressional majority symbolized the existence of political conditions for a rupture that had not been accomplished. The mass rally, in which the President, the ministers (including the military), and nationalistic and leftist leaders were joined, was the climax and the end of the rule of the masses as a technique for the retention of power and as a fundamental expression of populist democracy.

On the other hand, deep inside the nationalist model itself, or very close to it, the socialist model was constituted. It was present in the political organizations, in the modes of leadership, and in the techniques for action that sponsored the petroleum campaign, basic reforms, and nationalistic development, and it was active in the formulation of an independent foreign policy, in rural unionization, in the growing state control of the economy, in public opinion movements, and in cultural enlightenment. Therefore as the Left was entangled more and more in the techniques, modes, and aims of populist democracy, it could not succeed in freeing itself in time to propose and impose the alternative. In the continuing and increasingly deep familiarity with the rule of the masses, it finished by reversing the means and the ends, tactics and strategy, ideology and reality. For this reason it became submerged with the Coup d'Etat.

Yet again in the interior of the nationalist model itself the internationalist model was constituted. The deposition of Vargas in 1945, the exchange policies of the government of Eurico Gaspar Dutra in 1946-50, and the pressures that led to Vargas' suicide in 1954 were all events exemplifying this. The same can be said of another sequence of facts, since the analyses and propositions of the Cooke Mission in 1942 and the Abbink Mission in 1949 reveal the same general meaning. The *Programa de Metas* of Kubitschek's government (1956-60) perfectly demonstrated the practical development of the model of international association as an expansion policy of the Brazilian economy. The manner in which the automobile industry was created in the years 1956 to 1960 indicates a substantial alteration in the relations of the national economy with the international through the industrial sector. It must be remembered that other connections of various forms already had been established with the agrarian-export sector.

This picture of possibilities and dilemmas, particularly in 1960 to 1964, becomes more real when seen in the light of the following important political events of those years: the decoration of the Cuban Minister of Commerce and Industry, Ernesto "Che" Guevara, by President Jânio Quadros; the political crisis provoked by Quadros' resignation and the attempt to prevent the Vice President, João Goulart, from taking office; the rising political action of such organizations as the Institute for Research and Studies in the Social Sciences (IPES), the Brazilian Institute for Democratic Action (IBAD), the Radical Democratic League (LIDER), the Brazilian Auxiliary Patrol (PAB), the National Students' Union (UNE), and the General Workers' Confederation (CGT); the planned diffusion of the doctrine of revolutionary war as if it were being put into practice by the Brazilian Left; the obstinate continuation of relations with Cuba as a basic point of the independent foreign policy; the attempted coups d'état and the decree of martial law by President Goulart; the March 13, 1964, mass rally; the speech of President Goulart at a ceremony honoring him sponsored by the sergeants and non-commissioned officers of the Military Police the same year; the growing presence of the Left in political life.

The discussion of possibilities available becomes more real when we turn our attention to the economic situation. The crisis of events into which the economy was thrown, particularly after 1962, is fundamental. The economic crisis developed out of the structural crisis inherent in the form in which the national economy was seeking to reconcile the agrarian-export pattern with the nationalist developmental policy and the ever-broader association with international enterprises and organizations.

If it is true that economic development, institutional reforms, and cultural and political prosperity up to then had placed Brazil in a position to assume the stature and role of a second-class world power, it is undeniable that this position would necessitate drastic political operations. They were thrust upon the country with urgency precisely because of the manifestations and aggravation of the economic crisis. According to Celso Furtado's diagnosis:

> The exhaustion of the factors that sustain the industrialization process occurred apparently before the formation of capital reached the necessary autonomy in respect to the external sector. And this fact would appear to indicate that the difficulties confronting the country recently have a greater profundity than initially was suspected. There exists ample evidence that industrialization brought Brazil very close to that position in which development is a cumulative, circular process that creates by itself the means necessary to continue forward. In the case of Brazil this point will be attained when the obstacles in the ability to import are surpassed. The economy then will have reached that degree of differentiation in which investment orientation starts being a problem of economic options without the fiscal limitations of a rationed import capacity. It can be admitted that were it not for the sharp drop in imports and exports after 1955, Brazil would be about to attain this decisive point in the course of the present decade. Therefore this opportunity to enter into the restricted club of older capitalistic economies with a national autonomic

system apparently has been lost. Once lose, others forces are set in motion whose effects once again will make themselves felt. Thus, with the growth impulse once broken, the mechanism for the automatic control of consumption and capital formation that has been utilized successfully has been stagnated. Consequently, social problems begin to take on new dimensions, escaping the reach of instruments that have been used before with relative success.[7]

Data relative to the evolution of economic activities confirm important aspects of this image. That is, the dilemmas that confront populist democracy in Brazil are the result of the closing of a cycle of achievements of the nationalist model.

The favorable rate of growth of the gross national product registered between 1947 and 1961 began to decline in 1962, reaching a substantially reduced level in 1963. Especially elevated in the five-year period from 1957 to 1961, when it averaged almost 7 percent a year, the rate passed 7 percent in 1961 but fell to 5.4 percent in 1962. The estimates for 1963 indicate a growth of scarcely 1.4 percent and, moreover, a decrease of 1.8 percent per inhabitant.[8]

The importance of, and the urgency for, a decision are evident in the sphere of existing conditions and available possibilities. The Coup d'Etat took form and was executed on April 1, 1964. It was a politico-military operation destined to cleanse the arena for the broader and more effectual, that is, orthodox, execution of the internationalist model. Economic crisis and populist democracy showed themselves to be incompatible. For this reason "latent" political forces assumed supremacy over those formerly predominant. In the foreground military power appeared; however, one of the bases for the maneuver rested with the middle class.

PART III

THE NEW ORDER
AND STRUCTURAL DEPENDENCE

CHAPTER 9

THE COUP D'ETAT

The middle class was shown to be the class most docile to authoritarian solutions. Ever since the golden moments of the rule of the masses it was being prepared to submit to authoritarianism. In a large measure, the administrations of Ademar de Barros, Jânio Quadros, and Carlos Lacerda were manifestations of the rule of the masses in the heart of the middle class. The rule of these men was widely accepted on this social level. The studies of Francisco C. Weffort and Gláucio Ary Dillon Soares reveal and prove the connections between the variants of populism and the middle sectors of society.[1] The growing participation of these sectors in the Brazilian political process is an important fact in explaining some aspects of the "popular" success of antidemocratic reactions, especially the Coup d'Etat of 1964.

Thus there was an ample public opinion campaign directed especially toward the middle class that prepared the urban populations of São Paulo, Rio de Janeiro, and Belo Horizonte to accept in advance the overthrow of the government of João Goulart, the drastic modification of political institutions, and the complete reformulation of the economic policy. All these objectives were attained by means of a politico-military operation organized to combat communism and corruption, but involving at the same time economics and politics. The

THE NEW ORDER & STRUCTURAL DEPENDENCE

"March of the Family with God for Liberty" that occurred ten days previous to the coup prepared public opinion for that event and was reported in *Estado de São Paulo* of March 19, 1964, in the following terms:

> Yesterday the São Paulo capital had the greatest day in its history. In close formation and in perfect order approximately 500,000 democratically inspired people from all social levels constituting a veritable human torrent marched for two hours throughout the downtown streets, transforming the "March of the Family with God for Liberty" into the greatest civic manifestation ever seen in the four hundred and ten years of life in our metropolis.

According to the same newspaper, this was "the response of the *Paulistas* to the rally held six days previously in Guanabara." The paper was speaking about the manifestation of March 13, 1964, in a public square of downtown Rio de Janeiro attended by the President, the state ministers, nationalist and leftist leaders, workers, students, and intellectuals. Both acts were eminently political. The mass rally was to foment reform and was fully supported by the urban proletariat. The march was reactionary and was supported mainly by the middle class. The former was concerned with basic reforms and was a typical expression of populist democracy. The latter was preoccupied with Brazilian traditions (God, family, and 410 years of life in São Paulo) and was a manifestation oriented toward authoritarianism.

The participation of the middle class in politics is related to the progressive increase in their numbers due to the expansion of commerce — the tertiary sector. In fact, urbanization and industrialization have caused opportunities in service occupations, in business, in civil and military bureaucracy to multiply. Consequently the social groups in these fields become important in the political maneuvers of certain sectors of the dominant class. In a large part these are the masses that were given opportunities to grow under the administrations of Ademar de Barros, Jânio Quadros, and Carlos Lacerda. They are ambitious to rise socially at any price. Their cultural and mental universe is impregnated with dominant class values and patterns which are spread by television programs, movies, magazines, and newspapers. For this reason they see proletarian struggles and claims as a threat to their ambitions. Consequently they more easily become attached to the authoritarian solutions presented by some sectors of the dominant class. For large sectors of the middle class the democratic apparatus (especially the existence and function of Congress, state assemblies, and even municipal chambers) is tied to its financial expenses. At least they accept this argument. Thus at times they desire dictatorial schemes, and in this way they apply the brakes to the ambitions of the working class or its representatives.

Large sectors of the middle class develop economic and social ambitions on an increasing scale. It is exactly in the middle class that the "demonstration effect" exercises its deepest effects as a mechanism for consumption. This fact can be proved by the rapid appearance of dozens of advertising agencies, the growing consumption of television sets, and the spread of installment buying. In addition, the search for schools, particularly those on the secondary level, increases. Schooling, urbanization, and the growth of the tertiary sector are interconnected processes fundamental in explaining the importance of the middle class in the Brazilian political system. Data illustrating these tendencies are presented in Tables 17, 18, and 19.

129

TABLE 17

POPULATION DISTRIBUTION IN RURAL AND URBAN ZONES

Population	1940 (percent)	1950 (percent)	Index
Urban and surburban	31.2	36.2	5
Rural	68.8	63.8	−5

Source: Maria Thetis Nunes, *Ensino Secundário e Sociedade Brasileira* (Rio de Janeiro, ISEB, 1962), p. 117.

TABLE 18

LABOR DISTRIBUTION IN THE THREE SECTORS

Sector	1940 (percent)	1950 (percent)	Index
Primary	71.7	66.1	−5.6
Secondary	8.2	12.1	3.9
Tertiary	20.1	21.8	1.7

Source: See Table 17.

TABLE 19

GROWTH OF EDUCATION

Level	Number of Students		Growth Indices (1940 = 100)
	1940	1950	
Elementary school	3,205,753	5,108,924	159.2
Secondary school	155,588	365,851	235
Professional school or university	21,235	37,584	177

Source: See Table 17.

However, in explaining the political crises in Brazil the importance given to the middle class results in a large part from the growing discrepancies between middle-class ambitions and the actual possibilities of satisfying them. The progressive political awareness of the middle class arises from the fact that the quantitative growth of the middle class and the elevation of its demand patterns (indicated by secondary schooling, for example) were not accompanied by a corresponding increase in purchasing power.

This fact always was understood and was openly denounced by various sectors of the middle class, including the military bureaucracy. The "Memorial of the Colonels" directed to the Minister of War in February, 1954, contained important allegations in this respect. In that period a new scale for the minimum salary was being prepared by the Labor Ministry, whose director was João Goulart. Actually the minimum salary was to be increased 93.5 percent over the former one. It had been previously increased in 1951 by 230.5 percent. These alterations in the salary and wage scale were placing the middle class in a situation of inferiority in relation to other salaried groups. The elevation of the minimum salary of industrial workers was indirectly bringing about the reduction of broad sectors of the middle class to proletarianism. Inflation was still another factor working in the same direction but with greater vigor. Table 20 shows the increases in the minimum salary in São Paulo from 1940 to 1964.

In the face of this increase in the minimum salary, certain sectors of the military felt the progressive lowering of their standard of living. Inflation and the decrease of wage and salary differences between the working class and the middle class were causing the reduction of the latter to the proletarian level. This situation nurtured in an ever-increasing scale the political restlessness in civil and military sectors; at times this restlessness led to fundamental political events in the balance of civil power. An important document to clarify this aspect of national reality is the "Memorial of the Colonels," a section of which states:

The fixing of high wage scales for clerks with a university degree — wages that will double at the end of a few five-year periods — if it does not promote unjustifiable disparity between military and civilian employees will, by rushed amendments introduced into the houses of Congress without further examination of all its consequences, be able to lead only to another series of evils and inequalities within the military class itself. The elevation of the minimum salary to the level which in large cites will attain almost the maximum wages for noncommissioned officers certainly will result, if not corrected in some manner, in a deviant overthrow of all professional values, haulting any possibility of Army recruitment from the lower ranks.[2]

Unquestionably at this point the conditions of the middle class and the military were on a par. However, it is an unacceptable simplification to consider the increasing participation of the military in politics only on this level. The same military echelons, the so-called intermediary spheres, would turn out to be the active groups in the preparations for the military action of April 1, 1964.

The appearance of the military in politics is a normal occurrence in Brazilian political life. On the occasions of important historic events the military forces come forth as a decisive power to lead, to expedite, to control, or to expound the events. The movements, revolts, revolutions, and coups that marked the period after World War I cannot be understood without explaining the form in which the military forces participated in them.

TABLE 20

MINIMUM SALARY IN SÃO PAULO

Year	Salary (in Cr$)	Percent of Increase (Base: 1940)	Percent Relative to Former Salary
1940	220.00		
1943, July	275.00	25.0	25.0
1943, November	360.00	63.7	30.9
1951	1,190.0	441.0	230.5
1954	2,300.00	945.5	93.5
1956	3,700.00	1,582.0	60.9
1958	5,900.00	2,582.0	59.5
1960	9,440.00	4,191.0	60.0
1961	13,216.00	5,907.0	40.0
1963	21,000.00	9,445.0	58.9
1964	42,000.00	18,990.0	100.0

Source: Labor Ministry.

Political power and military power are theoretically autonomous. Decidedly they frequently appear to be independent in relation to the nation, economic classes, and social groups. But in critical situations they unite and are inseparable. In interpreting the role of the military element in the fall of the Empire, Oliveira Vianna emphasizes an important aspect toward understanding the way in which the military enters into politics. Reminding us that intelligent and systematic exploitation of the different military groups by civil petty politics was not exclusive of the Republic, he states:

Our civil politicians always turn to the Army as a field to exploit for their own interests: those of the opposition in order to rise to power; those of the government in order to keep it. Those who are on the bottom go to the barracks to dislodge those who are on top; these depend on the support of the barracks in order not to be dislodged by those on the bottom. And the real political function of the Army in our history has been this, the mere instrument of civil ambitions.[3]

Actually the increase of the military in politics is the result of the increase of tensions and antagonisms between economic groups and social classes struggling for power. This process becomes more accelerated and more facile when the democratic order and public opinion are less developed and less effective. The militarization of politics in general is a non-democratic form for the exercise of power. Artificial political parties and the weakness of the democratic conscience of professional politicians and citizens favor the transformation of military forces into a political party.

Probably none of the political events in Brazil after World War I were free from military participation. In some the military fulfilled a preponderant role, such as the coups d'état, which were always supported fully and ostensibly by military forces. The coups of 1937, 1945, 1955, 1961, and 1964 were all tied to the names of various military men. In every case the event had a particular significance. In all, moreover, we see artificial political parties and weak public opinion and democratic conscience. In reality, coups are the current forms for the succession to power in a society in which the rule of the masses and the oligarchies predominate over political parties. Under certain aspects the military coup is a crucial event through which all the weak points of the liberal model adopted in Brazil and in underdeveloped countries are revealed.

It is important to recognize that the military forces did not enter politics as a single massive body. They divided into as many currents as there are civil currents; yet they were able to act also in an autonomous manner and as a bloc. In general their acts definitely corresponded to the extremes of interests in civil political groups. For example, the national debate on the creation of the petroleum industry in Brazil symbolized perfectly the manner in which civil and military positions corresponded to, united with, and complemented each other. This is a necessary part of the political process itself.

In 1947 when the debate on the petroleum problem in Brazil became public, two generals were identified with or delineated the principal positions. General Juarez Távora proclaimed an "accommodation to national and foreign interests." Considering the same relations of the national economy with world capitalism, General Horta Barbosa adopted different conclusions. "Research, extraction and refining constitute parts of a whole whose possession ensures economic and political power. Petroleum is a resource for collective use, a creator of wealth. It is not admissible to confer on a third party the exercise of an activity that conflicts with national sovereignty. Only the state should exploit it in the name and in the interest of the highest ideals of the people." [4] This was the orientation that prevailed in the law that created Petrobrás six years later. It is important to remember, however, that the period from 1947 to 1953 was saturated with major political struggles involving students, the proletariat, elements of the middle class, the military, intellectuals, politicians, police, Standard Oil of Brazil, connivances, conciliations, and violence. [5]

It is clear that the military had their own goals in mind and visualized independent political action in opposition to civil politicians. In practice, however, their political actions only acquired direction within the domination and appropriation structure operative in the country. On a structural level military power appeared as the basis of civil power, interpreting it as a product of class relations. Frequently, as in the case of the Coup of 1964, the struggle against subversion and corruption involves an entirely new concept of the national historic process and foreign relations. The attempt was made to restore the integrity of political and economic powers that in the latter stage of populist democracy had become progressively dissociated. The implications of this can be clearly observed in the three documents quoted below.

March 20, 1964: I understand the worry and inquiries among my subordinates in the days following the mass rally on March 13. I realize that they are found not only among the General Staff of the Army and in dependent sectors, but also among the troops, in other organizations, and in the two other military bodies. I participated in them, and they were the reason for my conference with the Minister of War.

Two threats are evident: the advent of a Constituent Assembly as **a** means for the execution of basic reforms and the unleashing on a large scale of agitations generalized from the illegal power of the General Workers' Confederation (CGT). The armed forces were called upon to support such propositions.

In order to understand the problem some preliminary considerations are necessary.

The national and permanent military role is not properly to defend the government's programs, much less its propaganda, but to guarantee the constitutional powers, their functioning, and the enforcement of laws.

The armed forces were not instituted to proclaim their solidarity behind one power or another. If the option to stand behind programs, political movements, or holders of high offices was permitted them, then necessarily there would be the right also of opposition.

Relative to the doctrine that admits its use as a pressure force against one of the powers is the logic that also would be admissible to turn it against any one of them.

Not being a militia, the armed forces are not weapons for anti-democratic support. They are to guarantee the constructional authorities and their coexistence.

THE COUP D'ETAT

The ambitious Constituent Assembly is a revolutionary object for violence, its aim being the closing of the present Congress and the institution of a dictatorship.

Insurrection is a legitimate recourse for a people. It can be asked: Are the Brazilian people requesting a miliatry or civil dictatorship and a Constituent Assembly? Not yet, it would appear.

Will the armed forces enter into a revolution to deliver Brazil to a group that wishes to dominate it in order to command and countermand and enjoy power; in order to guarantee plenty in a pseudosyndicated group whose leaders live on subversive action each time more onerous for the public coffers; in order perhaps to submit the nation to Moscow communism? This certainly would be antipatriotic, antinational, and antipopular.

No, the armed forces cannot betray Brazil. To defend the privileges of the wealthy is in the same antidemocratic direction as serving fascist dictatorships or syndicalist communists.

The CGT announced that it will support the paralyzation of the country as a revolutionary scheme. A public calamity probably will occur. And there are those who desire that the armed forces remain outside of or servile to subversive orders.

The duty of the armed forces is neither one nor the other. It is to guarantee enforcement of the law, not allowing a movement of such gravity for the life of the nation because it is illegal. I have been dealing with the political situation to characterize our military conduct.

Besides the legal activity, the armed forces have exhibited a high understanding in view of the difficulty and actual detours of the present stage of Brazilian evolution. And they have remained, as is their duty, loyal to the professional life, to their destination, and, with continuing respect to their leaders, to the authority of the President of the Republic.

It is necessary here to stay always within the limits of the law; to be ready for the defense of legality; to be aware through the integral functioning of the three constitutional branches and through the enforcement of laws, including those that ensure the electoral process; and to be against revolution for the dictatorship and the Constituent Assembly, against the CGT, and against the discrediting of the historic role of the armed forces.

The most worthy Minister of War has declared that respect for Congress, elections, and the inauguration of the elected candidate will be ensured. He has, furthermore, declared that there will be no military pressure placed on Congress.

This is what I have to say in consideration of the worry and inquiries deriving from the present political situation and in respect to the current military conduct.[6]

March 31, 1964: There exists unquestionably in the country a climate of apprehension and worry in view of the action developed by some politicians who, with serious lack of respect for the existent political parties, seek to substitute them by juntas dominated by communists and who, to the horror of the law, insolently look to bring pressure on the powers of the Republic by union coercion through political strikes or strike threats. The prospect of a union dictatorship rises above the national community, contributing to the aggravation of inflation from which the Brazilian people have suffered so.

The mass rally of March 13 in the Brazilian Central Railroad auditorium summoned by the CGT and allied organizations, which confirmed the result of a suggestion made to Professor San Tiago Dantas by the communist leader, Luiz Carlos Prestes, in the former's interview in the A.B.I. (Brazilian Press Association) and published in the *Jornal do Brasil* on March 18, alarmed public opinion and established repercussions among the military. According to the words of various orators, it resulted in such aggravations to the legislative power that there was a virtual declaration of war on the armed forces that were loyal to the oath of defending the concordant and independent powers of the union — Law and Order. The military chiefs of the three armed forces saw with growing apprehension the development of a grave crisis of authority on all levels of the hierarchy, which in the passing days formed, along with the inflationary crisis, a vicious circle at once the cause and effect of the evils that overran the life of our people.

THE COUP D'ETAT

The ignominy of a communist-inspired union dictatorship is without doubt hovering over the Brazilian nation. Its audacious architects summoned the Congress in thirty days from the date of their ultimatum to attend to the request for the constitutional reforms contained in the presidential message under threat of resorting to "concrete methods," according to the expression of the notorious leaders of the CGT, not excluding the hypothesis of a general paralyzation of activities in the entire country. It is the same as if the malefactors, indifferent to the laws of the land and in an attitude of defiance to public authorities, should unite and proclaim the decision to attack certain property if they are not attended to within a definite length of time, in imitation of "your money or your life"! . . .

The communist-inspired union-strike system in the degree in which it strengthens and broadens itself becomes increasingly more dangerous for the nation's security.

I reaffirm to Your Excellency what some time ago I had already asserted — and I am certain that I am expressing the dominant opinion among the military chiefs — that the armed forces cannot share with any organization their constitutional attributes; the security of the government and of democratic institutions can rest only with the armed forces in their loyalty and military honor. The pacific coexistence of the military power with subversive union power outside the law is not possible in this area. . . .

With an authority that no one can deny, Lenin declared monetary inflation to be a precious ally of communism in capitalist countries, since it works silently and systematically in its favor. The leaders of this revolutionary syndicalism that controls various unions of essential activities and dominates spurious and markedly communistic organizations — CGT, PUA, CPOS, PAC, the Union Syndical Debate Forum (Santos), etc., which in directive No. 7 of September 15, 1963, to the Second Army I cited as poisonous serpents, enemies to democracy, traitors to the national democratic conscience — discrediting the high aims of healthy unionism as conceived by President Getúlio Vargas, appear to have adopted, consciously and sophistically, two lines of convergent action: deepening as much as possible the monetary inflation (which has brought such disgrace on the Brazilian people) and undermining the hierarchy and the discipline of the armed forces by an insidious action carried out systematically against the sergeants, corporals, soldiers, sailors, and marines.[7]

April 9, 1964: The Institutional Act that is decreed today by the Commander in Chief of the Army, Navy, and Air Force in the name of the revolution which saw victory with the support of almost the entire nation is designated to guarantee to the new government indispensable means for the work of the economic, financial, political, and moral reconstruction of Brazil in a manner in which it will be possible to confront in a direct and immediate way the grave and urgent problems upon which depend the restoration of internal order and the international prestige of our fatherland.[8]

As we can see, the overthrow of the João Goulart government on April 1, 1964, was based on the interpretation that the country was virtually involved in a revolutionary war, destined to install a syndicalist republic. President Goulart's relations with the union system and with nationalist and leftist political groups were considered as clear manifestations of a subversive program. It was the process of populist democracy attaining a level of development unexpected by the dominant class. According to Bilac Pinto:

In January, 1964, in contacts that I had with Governor Ademar de Barros and with politicians and the military, I gathered information on the arms distribution to the coastal and rural unions.

On the fifteenth of the same month, in a conversation with the accredited journalists in the Chamber of Deputies, I revealed the information that I had obtained in these meetings and after emphasizing the gravity of this new development in the march of governmental subversion, I urged the organization of a democratic movement against the coup in preparation, and counseled the civil population to arm themselves in order to resist.[9]

Preoccupation with the destiny of the political order and the economic and financial health of Brazil was not found exclusively among the opposition, the armed forces, and the government. It went beyond the national field under various forms. According to Edwin Lieuwen:

> The military coup against the Goulart government in Brazil in April, 1964, left Washington in a dilemma similar to the one it had faced in Guatemala a year previously, for although a constitutional government had been overthrown in Brazil, it was a government that had exhibited softness on the Communist problem and that had pursued notoriously unsound economic policies. Thus the Johnson Administration was quick to welcome a change. It was quite clear that the new administration had decided that Kennedy's attempts to impose democracy upon Latin America had proved fruitless and that in the future Washington would make a less passionate commitment to the principle of political freedom in Latin America.[10]

These considerations need to be complemented by remembering that already in previous years a reinterpretation of the foreign ties of Brazil in Latin America and in the Western world was taking place. In actuality the major world powers — the United States and Russia — were competing in the politico-military and economic spheres. Thus we see the importance of geopolitical concepts and particularly of a new interpretation of the transoceanic nature of American politics. Already in 1952 the then Colonel Golbery do Couto e Silva wrote:

> From an insular maritime power the United States has evolved into a major sea power increasing to the limit its coastal security zone. We find the definite recognition that there are no more oceanic strongholds and that escapist isolationism is dead and is

well dead; however, there are still some isolated voices in its favor, such as that of Herbert Hoover.

Now in such circumstances, when our Spanish-American neighbors openly oppose the United States under cover of the so-called Third Position or some other such label, thus profiting from North America's overseas preoccupations, Brazil appears to be in a favored position owing to its noncompetitive economy, its wide and proven friendly traditions, and above all its trumps to be played for a loyal bargain — manganese, monazite sands, the strategic position of the Northeast, the mouth of the Amazon with the island of Marajó — for a more expressive bilateral alliance that not only would assure us the necessary resources to contribute substantially to the security of the South Atlantic, but would enable us to defend, if the case arises, those extracontinental Brazilian areas involving North American territory so exposed and threatened by attack via Dakar-Brazil-Antilles; an alliance that would carry the recognition of Brazil's real stature in this part of the Atlantic Ocean, put in final form through a bifrontal policy and accommodation of our country and Argentina, both nations sharing equally against all reason and all evidence in weapons for naval warfare.[11]

According to various indications, this geopolitical interpretation of Brazil vis-à-vis Latin America and world blocs was utilized as the doctrine that shaped information for the overthrow of the Goulart government and its counterpart in foreign relations, the doctrine of revolutionary war. The government is concerned with reintegrating the political and economic systems on the level of world capitalism.

We can now see that the recent entry of the military into politics was not only to restore the principles of "hierarchy" and "discipline" that were being shaken in the armed forces, as set forth in the document of General Pery Constant Bevilacqua. Nor was it destined only to preserve the validity of "constitutional principles" and "harmony of power" such as was being debated in rising sectors of public opinion. The form in which the military forces engaged in the Coup d'Etat of 1964 was substantially different from their previous interventions. Even though the military itself had formulated its goals with full understanding of the cause, it is indisputable that the implications and developments of the coup confer a critical meaning to the event. If we place this fact within its structural and historical context, as well as against the political background of the period in which the coup occurred, we see that the coup involved a radical reverse in economic development and in the relations of Brazil with the world capitalist and socialist systems. To a large measure the coup represented a restoration of the internal and external ties that were in the process of being ruptured ever since World War I, especially during the Vargas epoch from 1930 to 1964.

Actually the coup was the termination of the long process of Brazil's transition from the sterling bloc to the dollar bloc. It is true that this process was well developed, as the analyses of Manchester and Normano indicate.[12]   However, the crises, tensions, and international conflicts centered on World War. I, the Depression, and World War II, besides other events, hampered the transfer of the hegemonic center of capitalism from Europe to the United States. After 1945 that country became aware of all the tasks inherent for supremacy in the capitalist world. Now the economic, political, military, and cultural missions that are its duty to support require great effort for the organization and mobilization of resources. For this reason the new mode of its leadership over Latin America was formulated only after the event, including such surprises as occurred with Fidel Castro and the victory of socialism in

Cuba. According to Edwin Lieuwen: "In their concepts of hemispheric economic cooperation, the Latin Americans and the United States were acutely divided from 1945 to 1959." [13]

However, starting with a given moment a new pattern of diplomacy was formulated. The doctrine that we live in "only one world" received a reevaluation, in which the social scientists were involved. The concept of total diplomacy concerned the fundamental spheres for existence of national bodies: political and military, economic and cultural. According to statements of the U.S. Assistant Secretary of State, Thomas Mann, and Herbert L. Matthews on different occasions and in different contexts:

> We can no longer live isolated from the rest of the world as if it did not affect vitally our national and individual well-being.[14]

No excuses are necessary for making a study of United States relations with Latin America. The importance of the region to us is only equalled, except for specialists, by our ignorance of it. It has been Latin America which impinged on our consciousness by such events as the Nixon trip, the revolutions in Venezuela and Cuba, and the unrest in the Caribbean.

Here is a world at our doorstep on which, to a considerable degree, we depend for our existence as a world power. If we were deprived of the raw materials of the area or its markets, our economy and security would be gravely — perhaps vitally — affected. It is an area where no hostile power can be allowed to gain a foothold for, strategically, this is our "soft underbelly." We cannot win the cold war in Latin America, but we can lose it there. Neutralism or an intense Yankeephobia could hurt us badly. A day will come when the Russians will make their bid for Latin America.

In terms of United States trade and investment, Canada and Latin America outweigh the whole rest of the world put together. Yet our foreign policy interests, expressed in the cold war, are directed far more to Europe and Asia. So we see the paradox of a financial and economic axis running north and south, and a political and military axis running east and west.[15]

In order to understand better to what extent the Coup d'Etat of 1964 was the termination of a succession of events (oriented toward accelerating the insertion of Brazil in "Western civilization" as an economic and political system) it is necessary to recognize that the industrialization cycle based on the substitution of imports had terminated. Especially as a model for nationalistic economic development fully supported on popular bases and implied in an independent foreign policy, the nationalist model had come to the crossroads.

Even in the period of the Kubitschek government and the Programa de Metas (1956-60) the pattern of association of national and foreign capital was put into practice, in addition to the facilities for independent foreign investment. During World War II the United States recognized that nationalism needed to be encountered in a realistic way in South American nations. We see this in a study by W. Feuerlein and E. Hannan dedicated especially to the perspectives offered them by the Latin American economy: "After 1929 several Latin American countries began to place their economic developments under their own control." [16]

For this reason the association of foreign and national capital is recommended as the best technique for coping with nationalism. In view of the evidence that the form which industrialization follows in Latin American countries could go against foreign economic and political interests, particularly those of the United States, W. Feuerlein and E. Hannan made some recommendations to businesses interested in investing in South America.

As was predicted in the first edition of this book (1941), foreign investors are observing that the combination of their capital with that of national investors in the receiving countries gives a certain degree of security against the excesses of economic nationalism.[17]

As we can see, the form being followed by the politico-economic rupture on which was based the transition of Brazilian society to an urban-industrial civilization was not compatible with foreign interests. Therefore, it was necessary to correct the manner in which Brazil was entering into the industrial era. Moreover, the Coup of 1964 was destined to give a new direction to the national historic process. According to Thomas Mann, quoted in the April 19, 1964, edition of *O Estado de São Paulo*:

> Last January when we assumed our duties we were convinced that communism would rapidly erode the government of João Goulart in Brazil. Even before assuming our actual position, moreover, we already were following a policy destined to grant aid to certain state governments in Brazil. We did not furnish any money to support the balance of payments or the budget, nor did we take any measures that could directly benefit the central government of Brazil. In our opinion, which I believe is shared by many Brazilian specialists, and in words attributed to efficient governors of various states, the limited assistance destined for the Goulart administration contributed toward financing democracy. . . . Now after the replacement of Sr. Goulart, if the government of Brazil supports a stabilization and self-help program, which is the type of development program that we want to see, or in other words, if they accept their responsibilities in the Alliance for Progress, we would be prepared to consider making appreciably more substantial funds available.

Upon assuming full leadership of the capitalist world in confrontation with the socialist world, the United States reformulated its relations with Latin America, especially

Brazil, upon whom new roles were conferred in the doctrine of interdependence. This situation acquired new connotations from consequences of the cold war that brought the United States and Russia to a tacit Treaty of Tordesillas. *L'Espresso* already had referred to the strange alliance resulting from the confrontation, interplay, and manipulation of the interests of the two super powers in different neutral countries. Because of the harsh ideological, political, economic, and military confrontations there was experienced "an absolutely new type of alliance, never before seen." [18]

To sum up, the Coup d'Etat of 1964 was a politico-military operation designed to achieve the following objectives:

a) Eliminate the risk of a seizure of power by the Left, or by extreme nationalist groups adept at an independent foreign policy and espousing the doctrine of Brazil as a power.

b) Control the negative consequences of inflation, restoring the technique of forced savings (inflation of income) and eliminating the mechanisms (rule of the masses) that make inflation function as increase of prices.

c) Reintegrate Brazil into the world capitalist system (Western civilization) by following the strategy based on geopolitics formulated as the foundation for United States leadership and the hypothesis of future all-out war.

d) Finally, and in synthesis, to restore the integrity and the integration of economic and political powers that were partially dissolved under the vigilance of populist democracy.

CHAPTER 10

THE STRUCTURAL DEPENDENCE

The Coup d'Etat of 1964 was not strictly a political or politico-military event. It had important economic roots and it was facilitated by economic processes that were forcing the termination of populist democracy. These processes can be synthesized as follows:

1) With the deterioration of exchange relations it became more urgent that Brazil enter a higher technical level of industrialization, in order to compete with other centers in the international market and to confront and surpass rapidly the barrier represented by the relative drop in the entry of foreign exchange.

2) The necessity of exporting manufactured products required the reformulation and elimination of protection that permitted or favored the creation and expansion of the industrial sector in the period when the policy of substitution of imports was in effect.

3) There was imposed a reformulation with the aim of placing Brazil in the international economy. The necessity for a high technical level requires growing association with organizations that monopolize the most modern technology in the most advanced industrialized nations. These organizations are the multinational oligopolies that maintain research laboratories and control technology. In reference to this Antônio Dias Leite has made some important observations.

THE STRUCTURAL DEPENDENCE

Nations that do not enter into an autonomous and programed technological and scientific development come always to depend more on developed nations for all products, processes, or equipment, or else copy the evolution of pioneering nations ten, twenty, or more years behind them. The delay depends directly on the time lapse for new discoveries and inventions to come into the public domain.

The delay will be less in the first case than in the second since the result will be obtained at the cost of greater direct participation by foreign enterprises in the national economy and, moreover, less capacity to regulate the direction and rhythm of economic evolution in the country.

In the second case a fuller control can be attained over the destiny of the economy itself, at the cost, however, of a permanent and large technological backwardness.

For both hypotheses there is manifested in the follower nations the necessity for continued importation of technology without any counterpart whatsoever in exportation, and the temporarily impassable distance between them and the creating nations is maintained. For some presently underdeveloped countries there is possibly a level of wealth that will facilitate the passing of this limit. The time interval needed to attain this liberating income level will vary from country to country. In the case of Brazil the task is possible and can be predicted in the not too distant future. Everything leads us to believe, however, that this level of income cannot be reached within the next decade. The objective in mind will be reached, on the other hand, with greater or lesser speed depending upon the greater or lesser priority given to investments in the field of education.[1]

Since the Brazilian people did not have the capacity to carry the politico-economic schism to its end, following the requirements of the nationalist model itself or a socialist alternative, their economic development came to depend again more and more on ties with foreign centers. Entrance into the stage of industrialization opened perspectives for an autonomous capitalist development. However, for this project to be effective a drastic reformulation of domestic and foreign structural ties was necessary—a reformulation that would have been possible on various occasions in the intermediate period from 1914 to 1964. The armed movements, the coups, and the revolutions that occurred in this period were indicative of the possibility for broadening and consolidating the autonomy. Moreover, the movements of the masses, populist democracy, nationalism, and federal leadership were concrete elements, and frequently effective ones, in this process. The nationalist model involved widening the structural ruptures. In addition, during these years the dominant political and economic systems were in crisis. The internal contradictions of world capitalism brought the termination of the leadership of England, France, and Germany. Step by step the hegemony of the United States grew and was consolidated in the capitalist camp, while that of the Soviet Union was strengthened in the social camp. This consolidation was witnessed only after World War II. The war actually was an important event for the integrated achievement of economic, political, military, and cultural leadership.

In the case of Latin America as a whole the hegemony of the United States is of long standing and traverses many phases, but in Brazil up to 1930 there were strong ties with England. The Depression, combined with the coffee crises, internal social movements, and the Brazilian Revolution of 1930, destroyed the most important ties with the sterling bloc. Afterwards Brazil took a decisive step in the direction of the dollar. A. K. Manchester pointed out that before 1930 the foreign exchange structure of Brazil already was being modified in a significant way to favor the United States. J. F. Normano reasoned in the following manner in giving a historic synopsis of Brazil in the decades preceding World War II:

British interests lost their place in Brazilian commerce and are losing their dominant position as suppliers of capital. Parallel to the change in principal products, New York replaced London in its importance in Brazilian economy and Wall Street took the place of Lombard Street. The entire postwar process of capital penetration by the United States in Brazil was a continuous process of expulsion and occupation of European positions, principally British ones.[2]

At the end of 1914 private American investments placed third in Brazil, after England and France. Thereafter the sum of capital, plus interest on direct investments, grew without interruption, as can be seen in Table 21. In this manner the foundation for interdependence was created.

In practice American investments were realized simultaneously with the reduction of England, French, and German participation. Thus new conditions for bilateral interdependence were constituted. It is obvious that the increasing authority of business interests and economic organizations in the Brazilian economy by only one country creates the foundation for intergrated interdependence, that is to say, political, military, and cultural, as well as economic, interdependence. In 1950 the United States already held more than 70 percent of the capital applied in businesses in Brazil. The data in Table 22 gives an idea of the structural significance of American interests in the country.

In later years the structure of these investments continued to develop. Moreover, the internationalizing process of the Brazilian economy acquired new connotations. The hegemony

TABLE 21

DIRECT INVESTMENTS OF THE UNITED STATES IN BRAZIL

(in millions of dollars)

Year	Amount
1897	1.0
1914	3.0
1919	4.0
1924	4.5
1929	108.4
1936	194.0
1940	240.0
1943	233.0
1950	644.0

Source: United Nations, *El Financiamento Externo de America Latina* (New York, United Nations, 1964), pp. 13 and 34.

TABLE 22

FOREIGN CAPITAL INVESTED IN BRAZILIAN COMMERCIAL
AND INDUSTRIAL ENTERPRISES

(as of December 31, 1950)

Country	Cruzeiros *(in millions)*	Dollars *(in millions)*
United States	17,792.0	950.4
United Kingdom	4,368.4	233.3
France	815.4	43.5
Belgium	810.4	43.3
Uruguay	727.2	38.8
Switzerland	250.3	13.4
Portugal	126.0	6.7
Sweden	65.0	3.4
Argentina	63.1	3.2
Netherlands	46.5	2.4
Other countries	72.1	3.8
Total	25,136.2	1,342.7

Sources: Bank of Brazil. United Nations, *Las Inversiones Extranjeras en America Latina* (New York, United Nations, 1955), p. 59.

of the United States over the nations of the capitalist world was consolidated and expanded and at the same time multinational organization developed. According to Paolo S. Labini, after World War II the competitive regime in capitalist economies was no longer prevalent: "Although it takes shape in various manners, in the modern economies the oligopoly is the most frequent market type." [3]

Frequently the importance of investment composition according to national origin of capital investors is merely formal. It is in these terms that we must understand the structure of foreign interests in the Brazilian economy after 1945.

The economic structure of Brazil had already been facilitating the predominance of national and international monopolistic organizations and techniques before that date. The inheritance by the twentieth century of a colonial-type economy with its base in coffee facilitated the formation of monopolies and oligopolies. The situation was often genuinely monopolistic. In 1942 Corwin D. Edwards of the Cooke Mission to Brazil made the following observations:

> In virtue of the relatively small volume of the Brazilian market for various industrial products and the official protection of commercial associations, the formation of national monopolies and agreements to restrict business presents probabilities of easier and more rapid development in this country than in the United States in its period of industrial formation. Between the two wars Brazil was considered by many international cartels as a marketing zone that these large enterprises divided up among themselves. Thus in certain sectors Brazil faced restrictions in international competition. . . .
>
> In Brazil corresponding legislation [antimonopolistic] was passed when an attempt was being made toward the creation of national enterprises seeking to free the country from colonial economic

THE NEW ORDER & STRUCTURAL DEPENDENCE

conditions. The Brazilian law was influenced also by socialist ideas that during the last decade have generated ample legislation destined to elevate the standard of living of the common man.

In a country where the large businesses, generally foreign, attempt to dominate the market, benefiting alien firms at the expense of small businessmen and local consumers, the preoccupation with the problem of industrial monopoly is the logical corollary to the growth of national consciousness.[4]

This means that in 1942 new sectors of the Brazilian economy already were linked completely with organizations whose policies were decided outside the country. Later there was rapid growth of international organizations. Referring to data published by *Desenvolvimento e Conjuntura* in May, 1961, Alberto Passos Guimarães points out the following:

In the competition between private national capital and private foreign capital the international monopolies carry a great advantage, since in the 66 businesses of greatest concentration (which hold 46.3 percent of the capital of the 6,818 companies in the study) 32 foreign businesses are prevalent, with a capital of 100.8 billion cruzeiros against 19 businesses or private national groups with a capital of 39 billion cruzeiros. . . .

A great number of large foreign enterprises have seen rapid expansion in recent years, jumping into the top positions in the order of size of capital because of generous concessions that were made to them (Directive 113, *cambio de custo*, etc.) by the state in the same way that they squeezed monopolistic profits from our country.[5]

Actually the entry of capital and technology on the side of expanding international organizations was occurring on a large scale. In this process Directive 113 of the Superintendency of Money and Credit (SUMOC) of January 17, 1955, played a relevant role. According to the stipulation of the first paragraph:

The Office of Foreign Commerce (CACEX) will be able to issue "import licenses without exchange cover" corresponding to foreign investments in the country for whole sets of equipment, or in exceptional cases for equipment destined to complete or perfect installations already in existence, when the Director of the Office is convinced that payment will not be made in foreign exchange.[6]

In reality the facilities conceded to foreign investors did not imply only "denationalization"; they involved the growing internationalization of the national economy. They implied an investment structure for the application of capital that was not always convenient to the equilibrium and functioning of the Brazilian economy. It was during this period that there was a concentration of investments in the automobile industry. The manner in which investments were made in this sector created various "competing" enterprises[7] for a relatively restricted available market. Moreover, other sectors important for the integration and general functioning of the system were

TABLE 23

DISTRIBUTION OF FOREIGN CAPITAL

(in percent)

Sector	1955	1956	1951	1958
Public services		0.10	0.01	0.19
Mining	11.92	11.71	2.43	0.48
Steel and metallurgy	11.42	15.48	8.13	1.07
Automobile industry	43.14	28.87	47.23	74.90
Construction materials	2.79	0.12	4.44	1.46
Textiles	3.29	12.55	7.71	0.68
Chemicals and pharmaceuticals	6.09	16.94	20.30	3.90
Lumber, rubber, etc.	8.12	4.34	4.94	5.56
Paper and cellulose	0.50	1.60	0.75	8.10
Food	7.36	1.40	2.93	3.41
Miscellaneous	5.37	5.43	1.10	0.19

Source: Bank of Brazil. Cf. "A Instrução 113 a Serviço da Indústria Automobilística," *O Estado de São Paulo*, August 13, 1959.

ignored. In Table 23 we can see how foreign capital was distributed after the SUMOC directive went into effect.

The benefits gained by international organizations and foreign companies were so broad and so rapid that the daily newspaper *O Estado de São Paulo* became worried about the denationalization of national industries and businesses. In 1961 the internationalizing effects of the economic policy were demonstrated in the Programa de Metas of the Kubitschek administration.

It is evident that when a foreign group is allowed to import capital goods equipment at the free market rate, it is placed in a privileged position in relation to national industry since the latter must buy "Promessas de Venda de Cambiais" at a higher rate. It is said that in the case of foreign groups the participation of new capital is concerned, which in spite of disadvantages for national industry is of major interest for the nation. We must emphasize, however, that in many cases these foreign investments do not signify actual participation of new capital but merely reinvestment of profits made in Brazil, partially a product of forced savings of the Brazilian people. In other cases the investments are made under the guise of old equipment (CACEX offers a wide margin of tolerance in the requirement for new material, and "bargaining" does the rest . . .) frequently extensively amortized before entering the country. . . .

It is suitable to study the influence of SUMOC Directive 113 on the denationalization of some of our industries, denationalization, that is, against the interests of our country. In recent years various Brazilian firms have seen themselves forced to accept the control of foreign groups since they could not bear the competition of these same foreign groups under the heading of reequipping. The only manner of survival was to accept the collaboration of foreign capital, which was frequently in majority control.[8]

Actually foreign economic groups predominate in economic

activities in Brazil. This fact is extremely significant because the predominance is indisputable in the secondary sector, exactly the most dynamic one. In a study of multimillionaire groups in the country, Maurício Vinhas de Queiroz arrived at important conclusions for a sociology of economic and political power. Considering groups with capital exceeding 4 billion cruzeiros, he disclosed that they are distinguished not merely for their greater economic and financial power, nor for their organizational complexity, but also for the leading role they play in Brazilian society as a whole. The conclusions of the study are summarized as follows:

1) Fifty-five groups of multimillionaires hold a strategic role in the Brazilian economy, occupying the leading positions in a succession of important business branches and thereby controlling a substantial part of the production and distribution of goods.

2) The multimillionaire groups are in the majority foreigners (52.7 percent). This is not the case with those in the 1-to-4-billion-cruzeiro capital range, where Brazilian groups predominate (65 percent).

3) As a rule the national multimillionaire groups existed before World War I, while the foreigners (there may be many exceptions) only entered more recently.

4) As for the sector of principal activity, 78.1 percent of the multimillionaire groups devote themselves to industry. In comparison with foreign groups, the national multimillionaires are outstanding in import-export businesses, banking, and the nondurable goods industry. The two groups are equal in the investment sector. In basic industries the national groups approximate the foreign groups. They have a definite disadvantage in distribution (especially petroleum), industrial services, manufacture of durable goods, and heavy machinery.

5) The foreign multimillionaire groups are composed for the most part of North Americans. Following these come the Germans,

English, and French respectively. The Americans show a preference for durable goods, principally automobiles.

6) Among the national multimillionaire groups, those of local origin are somewhat more numerous (exactly 58.3 percent) than those of nonlocal origin (Italian, Israeli, German, French, and Swedish). Disproportionately the latter are more inclined to industrial activities than the former.

7) There is no relation between the sector of principal activity of the groups and their secondary activity. Nearly every national group has at least one sector of secondary activity, while not all foreigners do.

8) The Brazilian national groups generally are much more diversified than the foreign groups. The extreme diversification of some groups, although irrational as to organization, has certain advantages in a market that is limited and subject to strong sectoral fluctuations.

9) More than half the multimillionaire groups have their headquarters in São Paulo, around a third in Guanabara, and only a small fraction in Minas Gerais.

10) The national multimillionaires have on the average twenty-one firms per group while the foreigners have barely eight.

11) As a rule, in the foreign groups the principal company is controlled 99 percent by the head office, but there are exceptions. In the case of national groups, the typical example is that of control exercised by a network tied to pure and mixed holding companies as well as by various individuals. By means of this network the decisions are handed down by the patriarch of the entrepreneurial family.

12) Half of the groups studied (50.9 percent) own pure holding companies. But their role is less than that of operating companies that work as a holding. In a large number of groups the leader company, although operating, has a large stock control in the associated firms.

13) Every foreign group is by definition managerial, while in the national groups the family of the entrepreneur and others related to him play an important part.

14) Scarcely 37.5 percent of the national multimillionaire groups

have no stock connection whatsoever with another group or foreign business.

15) Most frequently in the foreign groups the majority of directors are foreigners and the most important positions are occupied also by foreigners. There are cases, nevertheless, that differ radically from this pattern.[9]

The process of internationalization does not occur in a harmonic and systematic way. It depends quite a bit on international fluctuations, particularly the restructuring of the world capitalist system. As contradictions and crises persisted after World War II, the United States did not establish itself easily or completely as a world leader. Many events occurred before it did so. According to Arthur M. Schlesinger, Jr.:

During the war Nelson Rockefeller, as coordinator of the Office of Inter-American Affairs, began to develop the economic implications of the Good Neighbor policy, initiating the first technical assistance programs. It was an imaginative and promising start; but after the war it all lapsed (at least as a public effort: Rockefeller tried in various ways to sustain it himself privately). The United States government, preoccupied first with the recovery of Europe and then with the Korean War, forgot Latin America — a bipartisan error pursued with equal fidelity by the Truman and Eisenhower administrations. Between 1945 and 1960 the single country of Yugoslavia — a communist country at that — received more money from the United States than all Latin American countries put together.[10]

There is a constant interrelation between politics and economics in the critical moments of Brazil's foreign relations. Considered from a historic perspective, the fluctuations in these two spheres led to the Coup d'Etat of 1964. The coup was a fundamental political event in the execution of a new stage of relations between the United States and Latin America. A necessary consequence of this process was the destruction of populist democracy in Brazil.

Even in 1945 there was evidence of a conflict between the first manifestation of the incipient nationalist model for economic development and the requirements for United States leadership. Some Brazilian economic and political groups understood that the termination of World War II opened new perspectives for national development. The Teresopolis Economic Charter formulated at the Conference of Producers of Brazil (at a meeting in Teresopolis, May 1-6, 1945) summarized the principal aims of such development. This document created a complete balance of the principal economic, financial exchange, and fiscal methods whereby the government and the newer sectors of the dominant class hoped to bring the Brazilian economy to a new stage of expansion. Parallel to these debates the *queremista* movement gained support in the salaried classes, starting a popular basis for a developmental policy with populist democracy. *Queremismo* wanted a National Constituent Assembly with Vargas as President of the Republic. Before the end of the war and the imminent institution of the democratic order the country was preparing to develop its productive forces, increase the national income, and combat poverty.

Yet traditional domestic and foreign interests predominated, greatly frustrating the project. The more conservative sectors of the dominant class moved rapidly and Vargas was deposed on October 29, 1945. The merging of domestic and foreign interests was suggested also by Schlesinger in the following words:

More than anyone else, Berle provided the link between the Good Neighbor policy and the Alliance for Progress. His experience in Brazil, where he helped in 1945 to set off the train of events leading to the overthrow of the Vargas dictatorship, convinced him that the Good Neighbor policy could not survive as a diplomatic and juridicial policy alone.[11]

With the deposition of Vargas, the destruction of the Estado Nôvo, and the removal of power from the working masses, a different economic policy was inaugurated. During the government of Eurico Gaspar Dutra (1946-50) the foreign exchange reserves that had been built up during the war were permitted to be squandered unproductively. They were used for the importation of ostentatious consumer articles when it was possible and necessary to institute a program for the acquisition of machinery, equipment, and technology from abroad.

Despite this, however, some progress in the industrialization of the country was witnessed. The political basis of the nationalist model had been set up and was consolidated. The Social Democratic Party (PSD), the Brazilian Labor Party (PTB), and getulismo permitted one result, the uniting of bourgeois and proletarian forces. In 1950 Vargas was elected President of the Republic and took office in 1951. In 1953 he sanctioned the law that created Petrobrás, thereby instituting a state monopoly in the petroleum industry. On August 24, 1954, Vargas committed suicide.

The administration of Juscelino Kubitschek (1956-60) was a different and important stage. Again internal and external interests were merged. In his economic policy the nationalist model was abandoned and the developmental model of international association was put into execution. This was a fundamental stage for the internationalization of the Brazilian economy. The process can be seen more fully in the data contained in Table 24, where foreign investments and financing according to the country of origin are listed. It should be noted that the multinational nature of the economic groups confers new significance on these data.

TABLE 24

FOREIGN INVESTMENTS AND FINANCING [a]

(U.S. $1 million)

	1955		1956		1957	
	Investments	Financing	Investments	Financing	Investments	Financing
United States	12.0		24.3		61.4	
West Germany	7.1		17.3		8.7	
France	0.8		4.9		1.3	
England	5.1		2.0		6.4	
Italy	2.2		1.5		1.2	
Canada	0.5		0.9		2.7	
Switzerland	0.9		2.1		14.7	
Holland	0.7		1.3		0.2	
Belgium	0.2		0.2		3.4	
Japan					3.7	
Other Countries	1.8		1.2		4.5	
Total	31.3		55.7		108.2	

Economic evolution with modifications in economic policy orientation was achieved in the sphere of populist democracy. There was an ingenious reconcilement of internationalist economic policy with the rule of the masses based on nationalism. For this reason the years following were critical ones. Since the Kubitschek administration did destroy populist democracy, the internationalist model established itself, and the divorce between economic structures and power structures grew. Populist democracy became an increasingly unbearable or inconvenient obstacle. The dissociation between political power and economic power was accentuated.

At this period important motives entered into the picture, interfering with the foreign policy and the economic relations of Brazil. On one side was the problem of United States security vis-à-vis the Soviet Union and, more recently, Communist China. This is an important point in comprehending the form in which the doctrine of total diplomacy unfolded in the inter-

TABLE 24 – *Continued*

1958		1959		1960		1961	
estments	*Financing*	*Investments*	*Financing*	*Investments*	*Financing*	*Investments*	*Financing*
5.4	285.9	23.3	93.9	36.5	72.3	10.8	59.5
9.0	99.4	12.2	44.5	25.3	55.8	4.9	20.0
	13.9	8.1	25.9	6.6	30.1	0.7	11.5
0.9	3.0	4.0	21.2	3.2	10.4	1.9	3.6
0.5	19.6	3.3	30.2	2.9	34.5	0.9	8.7
0.3		0.8	0.9	0.1	11.6	9.1	
0.6	0.3	5.6	2.4	9.1	0.2	4.6	4.6
0.2	6.8	0.7		2.7		1.4	
0.5	0.1	1.9	0.3	1.3	4.1	1.7	0.1
0.2	26.2	3.3	99.0	8.1	1.1		10.8
4.9	52.2 b	2.6	44.9	11.0	82.7 c	3.2	9.3
2.5	507.4	65.8	369.4	106.8	304.9	39.2	130.2

Source: Report from SUMOC. Cf. *15 Anos de Política Econômica no Brasil*, document prepared by the Center for Economic Development (CEPAL-BNDE) (Rio de Janeiro, 1964), p. 52-C.

a Of specific projects registered with SUMOC.

b It is worth noting that of this amount the portion coming from Poland was U.S. $20.1 million.

c The high amount in the "other countries" category for 1960 is due principally to Yugoslavia ($15.5 million), Czechoslovakia ($12.2 million), Sweden ($11.8 million), Spain ($11.0 million), and Denmark ($10.1 million).

nationalization of the Brazilian economy. Some documentation will illustrate the different connections between the economic, political, and military aspects of this problem.

The main objectives of the United States with respect to Latin America are fundamentally set by the need to ensure the security of all those points from which an attack could be launched against the United States, and by the need to maintain an adequate supply of the raw materials that are critically needed by the United States both in peace and war. Subordinate to these, it has also become an American objective to deny certain strategic materials to the Soviet Union and the countries associated with it; and to obtain the political co-operation of the Latin American republics in the United Nations and elsewhere. These objectives have called for a broad policy designed to increase the internal stability of a region that is so important a part of the free world. . . . Thus, a main interest of the United States is to have available, in any future global conflict, adequate military bases to defend the Panama Canal and to maintain other lines of communication throughout the hemisphere. Moreover, since the United States had to furnish more than a hundred thousand troops to defend military bases in Latin America during the Second World War, it also has an obvious interest in seeing that effective local armed forces would be available to assume this duty in any future global conflict. For this purpose and others, the standardization of arms and training throughout the hemisphere is an evident desideratum. Finally, the United States has an interest in the Latin American ability to contribute troops for collective action against aggression, as in the United Nations action in Korea, for which only Colombia was able to contribute troops.[12]

To this writer, an implacable criterion of judgment has to be that of the safety of the United States. The fact that a new order is different or unfamiliar to us is wholly secondary in importance to the question whether it is, in the context of the prevailing world struggle, dangerous to our own survival. The United States can, and during most of its existence has, coexisted quite happily with all manner of social systems governed by all manner of political organization. It is, for example, quite possible to imagine systems not based on the institution of private property (though we might be dubious about their success), and for the United States to work happily with them — provided they do not assert as a necessary concomitance that they must join with others in conquering the United States, or insist (as Castro does) that they will, in some fashion, attack the American political-economic system. For a period of nearly twenty years, the Soviet Union has coexisted with Finland, whose system bears no relation at all to the Communist system — being assured that a non-Communist

Finland represented no danger to the safety of the Soviet Union. But she would not tolerate Finland's entry into, or association with, NATO.[13]

In this context one can place the political, economic, and military relations of Brazil with Latin America and the United States. The Coup d'Etat of 1964 particularly was an occurrence that formed part of the general process for the establishment of a new concept of "Western civilization." Referring especially to the Brazilian situation, Senator Wayne Morse, chairman of the Senate committee for Latin America, asserted the following:

The benign American attitude toward Latin American military regimes has just helped Argentina to see itself dispose of a constitutional government. The aid that the United States extended to the juntas of the Dominican Republic, Guatemala, Ecuador, Honduras, and El Salvador helped unleash the coup of Castello Branco in Brazil. When we rush to approve and supply the Castello Branco junta with new and vast sums, we strengthen the Argentine military class in seizing control of their government. It was cited that the Argentine military interpreted that the American support to the Brazilian military junta signified that formal American opposition to a coup in Argentina was purely for the sake of appearances. They are right. It is only purely for appearances. We have demonstrated by means of our actions in the last three days that it was purely for appearances. We have little interest in constitutionalism. It may be for that reason that what our military missions are teaching Latin Americans is encouraging and not discouraging their coups against constitutionalism.[14]

Parallel to this, dealings and associations between national and foreign enterprises were developing. The pattern inaugurated in the period of the Kubitschek administration progressed greatly. It would appear that economic, political, and military power are autonomous. In practice, however, they are linked in various ways. According to observations by Lincoln Gordon and Engelbert L. Grommers continuing the studies of W. Feuerlein and E. Hannan, the association of companies is a practice typical of the post–World War II period. And the reasons are at the same time economic and political.

The motives for a U.S. company to engage in a joint venture are partly of a "business" and partly of a "political" nature. The principal "business" elements are that partnership reduces the capital outlay required in the foreign project, and that cooperation with a local industrial group provides the investor with the know-how required to operate under the specific local conditions. In ideal cases, this may enable him to get off to a "flying start," especially when the local partners have previously been engaged in the manufacture of similar products, have production facilities and a reservoir of managerial and technical personnel, and have established distribution channels and a certain amount of goodwill and product acceptance. The "political" motives are based on the assumption that a partnership arrangement with a local industrial group or local individual shareholders may offer some protection against nationalist pressures of one or another variety. . . .

The number of Brazilian-owned enterprises that are potential partners has increased considerably in comparison with the prewar period.[15]

Seen in the light of multinational oligopolies, these developments created crucial problems for the interpretation of new conditions of economic progress in Brazil. In this period of history the interrelationships between politics, economics, and the military became more complex, blunting conventional interpretations. The very concept of "nation" entered into question when the economic and political processes were linked between continents.

Again we see the necessity to formulate a doctrine of interdependence in which is inserted the doctrine of reversal of expectations which formed the basis of the domestic policy of the rulers after April, 1964. In confrontation with the autonomous economic development model and an independent foreign policy, Castello Branco's administration put the pattern of interdependence into practice. His administration was concerned with negating the nationalist model in practice and in theory. For this reason the agreement guaranteeing private investments signed by United States and Brazilian representatives in February, 1965, is a fundamental and symbolic document. It dealt with a logical development in the spirit of the Alliance for Progress. A uniform system of investment guarantees established by the agreement is intended fundamentally to "promote conditions to stimulate the flow of foreign investments that contribute to the increase of capital resources in the participating countries." [16]

In this manner the multinational oligopolies assumed increasingly important roles in economic policy decisions, and the conditions for the organization and development of the Brazilian economy were modified substantially. While examining the relevance of this new situation for all Latin American peoples, Celso Furtado affirms the following:

Invited to act in Latin America with a series of privileges outside the control of United States antitrust legislation, and with the politico-military protection of that country, the large American companies must necessarily transform themselves into a super-power in any Latin American country. Since a large portion of basic decisions in respect to investment orientation, localization of economic activities, technological orientation, research financing, and degree of integration of the national economies falls to them, it is perfectly clear that the decision-making centers represented by the different nationalities will pass into an increasingly secondary level.[17]

This is the historic context in which we can see the transition from an independent foreign policy and autonomous economic development to a doctrine of interdependence and internationalistic development. Beginning on April 1, 1964, the Brazilian government chose decidedly for the doctrine of interdependence in all its implications in the sphere of Western civilization. In this manner economics and politics, as well as the military and the cultural, are linked once more and in a different way. In regard to this choice the statements of Castello Branco and Juracy Magalhães are clear.

To pursue the national objectives, two options were proclaimed as compatible with the preservation and expansion of Brazilian autodetermination: a policy of independence or a neutral position. The expression "policy of independence" has been distorted and has lost descriptive usefulness. It was presented as an inescapable innovation, ignoring the fact that the concept of independence is operational only within determined practical considerations.

It is an objective, not a method. In the present context of bipolar power confrontation with radical divorce of ideological political positions between the two centers of power, *the preservation of independence presupposes the acceptance of a certain degree of interdependence, whether in the military, the economic, or the political arena.*

No country, be it in the Western world, be it in the Soviet world, would be able to defend itself alone against one or other of the power centers. The defense must be essentially associative.

Similarly in the economic field the recognition of interdependence is inevitable, not only in commerce, but in everything touching upon investments. Independence is a terminal value. Instrumentally it is necessary to recognize a certain degree of interdependence in which it is not necessary to carry to the breaking point commercial and financial contacts with countries of different political and economic systems.

In its foreign policy Brazil cannot ignore the fact that we made

Finland represented no danger to the safety of the Soviet Union. But she would not tolerate Finland's entry into, or association with, NATO.[13]

In this context one can place the political, economic, and military relations of Brazil with Latin America and the United States. The Coup d'Etat of 1964 particularly was an occurrence that formed part of the general process for the establishment of a new concept of "Western civilization." Referring especially to the Brazilian situation, Senator Wayne Morse, chairman of the Senate committee for Latin America, asserted the following:

The benign American attitude toward Latin American military regimes has just helped Argentina to see itself dispose of a constitutional government. The aid that the United States extended to the juntas of the Dominican Republic, Guatemala, Ecuador, Honduras, and El Salvador helped unleash the coup of Castello Branco in Brazil. When we rush to approve and supply the Castello Branco junta with new and vast sums, we strengthen the Argentine military class in seizing control of their government. It was cited that the Argentine military interpreted that the American support to the Brazilian military junta signified that formal American opposition to a coup in Argentina was purely for the sake of appearances. They are right. It is only purely for appearances. We have demonstrated by means of our actions in the last three days that it was purely for appearances. We have little interest in constitutionalism. It may be for that reason that what our military missions are teaching Latin Americans is encouraging and not discouraging their coups against constitutionalism.[14]

Parallel to this, dealings and associations between national and foreign enterprises were developing. The pattern inaugurated in the period of the Kubitschek administration progressed greatly. It would appear that economic, political, and military power are autonomous. In practice, however, they are linked in various ways. According to observations by Lincoln Gordon

and Engelbert L. Grommers continuing the studies of W. Feuerlein and E. Hannan, the association of companies is a practice
typical of the post–World War II period. And the reasons are
at the same time economic and political.

The motives for a U.S. company to engage in a joint venture
are partly of a "business" and partly of a "political" nature. The
principal "business" elements are that partnership reduces the
capital outlay required in the foreign project, and that cooperation
with a local industrial group provides the investor with the know-
how required to operate under the specific local conditions. In
ideal cases, this may enable him to get off to a "flying start,"
especially when the local partners have previously been engaged
in the manufacture of similar products, have production facilities
and a reservoir of managerial and technical personnel, and have
established distribution channels and a certain amount of goodwill
and product acceptance. The "political" motives are based on the
assumption that a partnership arrangement with a local industrial
group or local individual shareholders may offer some protection
against nationalist pressures of one or another variety. . . .
The number of Brazilian-owned enterprises that are potential
partners has increased considerably in comparison with the prewar
period.[15]

Seen in the light of multinational oligopolies, these developments created crucial problems for the interpretation of new
conditions of economic progress in Brazil. In this period of
history the interrelationships between politics, economics, and
the military became more complex, blunting conventional interpretations. The very concept of "nation" entered into question
when the economic and political processes were linked between
continents.

Again we see the necessity to formulate a doctrine of interdependence in which is inserted the doctrine of reversal of
expectations which formed the basis of the domestic policy of

struggle for basic reforms and the reconcilement of traditional sectors of the dominant class; the redefinition and growth of culture and national consciousness on one hand and the preservation and broadening of alien ties on the other. This is the general picture, complex and frequently contradictory, in which progress was taking place. In this context and in this manner the political, cultural, and economic development can be seen. And it is in this same context that the Coup of 1964 and the reorientation of the Brazilian enlightening process occurred. Actually this process was interrupted and led in another direction with the following:

a) Economic progress placed Brazil in the position of an independent nation with strong influence over Latin America and Africa. In this case the "Brazilian model" of development would be an inconvenient model for other dependent nations of the third world, besides directly hindering United States leadership on the South American continent. Moreover, the conduct of Brazil in relation to socialistic Cuba already was deeply hurting the harmonious point of view desired by the Organization of American States.[1]

b) The rule of the masses and leftist nationalism in the field of populist democracy threatened the power of the dominant class. The eventuality of political crises associated with economic crises would open the way for socialism. In fact, revolutionary events surged forth on various occasions, as in 1945 with Vargas' deposition; in 1954 with Vargas' sulcide; in 1961 with Quadros' resignation; and in 1964 with Goulart's deposition.

c) The United States assumed full political and economic leadership in the capitalist world. In the interplay of the cold war with the Soviet Union, the areas of influence and dominance of the two nations were defined. As a consequence Latin

America as a whole remained under the aegis of the former. On this subject the study of Arthur M. Schlesinger, Jr. (under the Kennedy administration) made some suggestive revelations:

> Latin America de Gaulle freely acknowledged as a primary American responsibility, but he asserted that common cultural ties gave France a particular access and role; Kennedy said he welcomed French contributions to Latin American development.[2]

> As we considered Latin America primarily our own responsibility, so we considered Africa primarily a Western European responsibility.[3]

> Indeed, he [Kennedy] was the first American President for whom the whole world was, in a sense, domestic politics.[4]

This is the over-all context for the shift to a doctrine of interdependence and, simultaneously and necessarily, to a policy of reversal of expectations. In this sense the reversal of expectations, proclaimed by the government inaugurated in 1964, transcended the economic sphere and was projected into a political and cultural orbit. For this reason the Coup d'Etat of 1964 represented an important alteration in the enlightening process in Brazil. With the government of Castello Branco was begun a complete program of reformulation of valid institutions in a way to adjust the expectations and ideology of different social classes to the status quo. This aim progressively altered the financial and economic, exchange and fiscal, and political and educational institutions.[5] It reintegrated the political and economic powers that had been partially dissociated during the period 1961-64. Castello Branco outlined his policy as follows:

> The new government policy came to encompass two plans of action; the first, and the more immediate, was correction of the

deformations which appeared in all manifestations of the Brazilian developmental process, considering it in an organic sense, which included political, military, economic, social, and foreign aspects; the other was the adoption of a strategy for unleashing a progress spurt equally and in an integrated sense, taking into consideration the Brazilian situation in its entirety.

The first step of this policy for national reconstruction consists obviously in the restoration of order in all areas and of authority following the constitutional principle.

The elimination of systematic deformations, with the objective of improving the functioning of existent institutions, determines the change of methods of action, with the purpose of seeking objective solutions for problems in place of adopting palliatives and creating demagogic slogans. On the other hand, with the goal of preparing adequate institutional structures for the eruption of a new progress spurt and the construction of a new Brazilian society, the perfectioning of institutions is necessary by means of democratic reforms, realistically conceived.[6]

The policy of the revolutionary government has been exactly that of supporting the reorganization of national power; restructuring the economy and finances of the country; establishing new institutional means; logically organizing the administrative apparatus; joining again democratically students and workers; and adjusting the wages of the armed forces.[7]

Once the preliminary military and political operations were accomplished, bringing the downfall of the nationalist model of development and with it populist democracy, the new rulers decided to establish other patterns of economic and political conduct. They planned to replace the values and patterns of *pioneer capitalism* of nationalist shading with the values and patterns of *mature capitalism*, conspicuous and ascetic. Based on a strictly mechanical conception of social relations, and particularly of economic conduct, the doctrine of reversal of expectations was formulated by the Minister of Economic Coordination and Planning, Roberto de Oliveira Campos. It was conceived as one of the fundamental theories of governmental economic policy. The doctrine was concerned with surging the economic system, and consequently transforming it through the requisites that the Minister envisioned and presented as being based on the theories of Max Weber. In one of his formulations the doctrine appears in the following terms:

The present government does not propose to be pleasant to everyone. It proposes to follow what the circumstances dictate, keeping in mind not the interest of groups or classes but the success of over-all objectives, such as the strengthening of our national power, the implantation of firm bases for development of free enterprise, the correction of social injustices, the integration of the Brazilian market, the adjustment of institutions to the new political, economic, and social situation of the country. . . .

It is not easy to change habits or attitudes. Even less so when those habits and attitudes come from people profiting from inflation. The problem, however, is not the immediate convenience of the few who are benefiting from inflation. The great challenge that the government and the entrepreneurial and salaried classes have to confront is not that of saving this or that isolated business, but that of re-creating conditions in order that free initiative may hold an economic meaning and a social meaning in our country — an economic meaning that allows it to develop without crises and disturbances, generating stable employment and truly national wealth; a social meaning that allows it to respond to anxieties, legitimate and nondeferrable, for the integration of the urban and rural masses for the benefits of economic development.

After a year in power the government of Marechal Castello Branco has corrected the principal distortions that obscured an objective vision of the paths to be followed, and the victory over inflation becomes not only viable, not only possible, but frankly probable. The workers themselves already believe it and are beginning to support the phase of reversal of expectations and price stabilization as payment of their share of required sacrifices. The compliance of hundreds of businessmen with the terms of Directive 71, a compliance that will multiply with required simplifications in this directive, indicates also that the greater part of Brazilian businessmen discern perfectly the meaning of the governmental action and the meaning of their own role in the economic context of the country.

We have arrived, however, at the decisive moment in which the old customs of an entire generation corrupted by the distortions of inflation must be abandoned. As the President of the Republic stressed a month ago in his speech on the installation of the Planning Advisory Council (Conselho Consultivo de Planejamento), "We must conquer the fatalism of the consumer who believes in the inevitability of rising prices and to which he submits passively, instead of bargaining with the suppliers and rewarding the cheapest; we must conquer the indifference of the producer to quality and costs, accustomed to selling everything, and transferring the costs to the consumer unheedful of efficiency and protected against competition by the exacerbation of inflationary demand; we must clarify the illusion of the salaried worker, seduced by the promise of high nominal salaries, greater than the actual possibilities of the economy and for this reason immediately weakened in the tragic price spiral; we must avoid the frustration of the one who would save money but who sees his money devaluating and decides in favor of consumption, speculation, or exportation for his money, this in a country so in need of productive investments; we must denounce the carelessness of the luxury consumer who affronts the hopelessness of the needy with his extravagance and frivolity, and who in a poor country exhibits wealth incompatible with a feeling of social solidarity and the urgency of concentrating all possible resources on productive investments capable of accelerating development." [8]

In this conception the interests of the workers and the entrepreneurs are by definition congruent and harmonious. Consequently, the modifications in their conduct and mentality can and must go together. Based on a mechanical interpretation of social relations in general (and principally economic relations), rhetorical formulas insupportable by modern social sciences are presented by Roberto Campos. Thus, without taking into account the conditions, the factors, and the tendencies of the whole refining process that develops during the transition of an agrarian civilization to an urban-industrial civilization, he verbally gets rid of patterns and techniques, values and concepts. To his way of thinking the actual situation appears similar to a game of men on a checkerboard. He combats nationalism, the rule of the masses, the experiences of state rule, and the role of protective tariffs as if these events were episodes or fables. In a passage typical of his manner of interpreting the social situation, Campos affirms:

They are the myths, and even more the lies, that afflict our economic conduct and distort our political situation. We capitalize in myths, some of them in the hope that their identification will be the beginning of an urgent process of *Entzauberung*, or disenchantment, by the return to reality, such as is referred to by Max Weber. Then if the aims of society can be wrapped in mysticism and magic, their means and methods must be rational and effective.[9]

However, the doctrine of reversal of expectations is not an invention of the Minister, nor does it refer only to economic life. It involves different levels of national existence. It is a verbalization to impart meaning to the drastic alteration of political, economic, and cultural development in Brazil. We must consider that this doctrine was formulated simultaneously and congruently with the fight against (1) the conquests of populist democracy, (2) the growth of cultural enlightenment, (3) the increase of theories and currents in politics, (4) industrial development, (5) the fight against poverty (6) new techniques for teaching literacy, (7) the political and spiritual emancipation of growing sectors of the national population, (8) the execution of an independent foreign policy, (9) the the adoption of multilateral international obligations. If we take all these manifestations of the Brazilian enlightening process into consideration, we discover that the reversal of expectations is an ironic and cruel euphemism.

What actually is planned is the over-all reorientation of the political and economic process in thought and action. This reorientation is designed to apply a new concept to the Brazilian economy. It is concerned with the country placing itself (as far as international economic relations and consequently, domestic ones go) on the same footing as more industrialized and dominant nations. According to the new government of April 1, 1964, the country must substitute the inferiority complex inherent in nationalism with a superiority complex inherent in the official formulation of the doctrine of interdependence. For this reason foreign competition and cooperation become natural and desired variables in the governmental economic policy. In other words, the "sacrifice" of Brazilian companies is analyzed by the rulers as an inevitable result of confrontation between different business mentalities and different technical capacities of organizations. The increase in the indices of bankruptcy and creditors' agreements of Brazilian firms or their association with foreign enterprises was faced from this point of view.

Some companies actually have shut their doors and others in the near future will be obligated to cease activities. If we examine the cases individually, we will see that the majority of the companies were obligated to close their doors owing to managerial incapacity or inability to adjust to the economic conditions required by the country.[10]

Those responsible for the government's financial and economic policy have been worried by the industrialists, who, satisfied with profits obtained principally because of exchange and tariff protections, were not interested in improving their productive activities. Free from any competition in the domestic market and producing for a not very changing demand, they were not motivated to produce more or to improve quality and decrease costs.

The transfer of merchandise from the Special Category (in which the requirements were greater for importation) was one of the means adopted to create this necessary change in the businessman's mentality. It is planned that the competition of foreign merchandise, or at least the possible competition, will force a lowering of domestic prices, which are much higher than necessary, and will encourage industries to improve methods of production and attain higher levels of productivity.[11]

In a country with a long history of independence, of continental dimensions such as Brazil, with already highly developed regions, a fear of colonialism shows an unjustifiable inferiority complex, a misunderstanding of the paths of history, and an underestimation of our own worth. We can and we must attract the collaboration of foreign technology and capital without granting them any privilege, requiring full compliance with our laws, but also without resentment and without fear, since our own history reveals that São Paulo, the region that absorbs more foreign capital than any other in the country, far from being denationalized, has been transformed into a factor of national saving, and today exports investors and technology to the Northeast, and resources, technology, and business organization to the Amazon region, which constitutes a true cement for binding national integration.

Healthy nationalism that benefits businessmen, that benefits the government, that benefits the nation, is that which seeks organization and effectiveness of investments, whether internal or external, in the conviction that true independence comes from the energy that is put toward achieving the national program and not that of demagogues who want the alienation of patriots and seek to place the blame for our normal shortcomings on others.[12]

This entire doctrine is formulated in the name of various combinations of doctrines: pragmatism and Weber, social peace and militarization of politics, economic development and a catastrophic concept of relations between peoples. In essence it looks for optimal integration between economics and politics in a monolithic power structure. In this manner it plans to make use of, and accelerate the diffusion of, "rational" patterns of organization of economic and political relations found in the more developed capitalistic centers. In the eyes of the government, and especially in the thinking of Roberto Campos, the national situation is arbitrarily reduced to a synchronic totality in which conduct, institutions, and social techniques are manipulated as if one were dealing with an arithmetic problem.

Basically the government program and the concepts, particularly in the form that Roberto Campos has given them, are logically and historically inadequate. They do not relate to contemporary Brazilian society in its economic, political, or cultural processes. They represent a national situation, following a model that was not historically constituted in Brazil. They consider theoretical and logical categories for a universe significantly foreign to Brazilian history. In playing with theories and myths, the economist substitutes one for another without reflecting on their historical nature and their cultural implications.

These practical and theoretical questions are not of interest merely for an analysis of the Brazilian situation as it shaped up after 1964; they are common to all countries belonging to the third world, that is, those in cultural dependence. Making particular reference to Latin America, the economists Aníbal Pinto and Osvaldo Sunkel diagnosed the origins of many errors current in economic policies adopted by Latin American nations:

> The majority of young economists who study in the university centers of industrialized countries return to their own environment with theoretical schemes dissociated in a greater or lesser degree from objective reality and from the problems of their nation of origin, and frequently with operating tools that cannot be fruitfully employed. It is not unusual, then, that upon their return they must pass through a period of "agonizing reappraisal" in a desperate attempt at readaptation. The more mature and intelligent separate the chaff from the wheat, establishing a true orientation for their theoretical abstractions and selecting their tools according to the possibility of their usefulness. Others, however, fall into the well of confusion and despair, or are transformed into repeaters of didactic clichés or mathematical acrobats, while they reveal themselves to be impotent in interpreting the national situation and even less in aiding the resolution of economic problems.[13]

In synthesis the economic policy put into execution in 1964 is not a program for economic development. It is oriented toward modernizing the economic system of Brazil. It is a policy designed to perfect economic relations and institutions. On a domestic level its functioning must be guaranteed without the risks of tensions generated or aggravated by such structural transformations as become urgent or are imposed upon economic institutions. On a foreign level it is necessary to guarantee the integration of world capitalism and facilitate the movement of production factors. In particular, modernization is patterned to guarantee the functioning of the process of greater capital formation without the obstacles of protective exchange rates, tariffs, and fiscal policies or ideologies.

CHAPTER 12

DICTATORSHIP

It was necessary to formulate a new power structure, since the requirements of a new economic policy, of a reversal of the direction of cultural and political development, led to other techniques and modes of leadership and action. The civil and military powers were fused into a single power which was concerned with "purging" the institutional system in order to unite it with the demands of newly assumed obligations by the national society, both in itself and with foreign policy-making centers. In this sense the future is conceived as the perfected present. The future is the purified status quo.

Foremost it was necessary to formulate and put into practice a new mode of leadership. This was one of the dilemmas that faced those who assumed power on April 1, 1964. The fight against the experiences and the inheritance of populist politics, particularly nationalism and the Left, required new definitions, because the new leaders did not have charisma or popular appeal. Moreover, as the revolutionary motives were quite rational, the new government insisted upon the negation of charismatic leaders and demagogues. It proclaimed the organization, responsibility, and efficacy of the government as if collective reasons were immediately reducible to mechanical relations. The profit principle needed to be transformed into the collective morality. It was planned to institute a theoretically possible rationality, confusing theory with practice, abstract possibilities with concrete possibilities, Max Weber with Benjamin Franklin. In short, this concept was presented initially in the following words of Roberto Campos, Marshal Humberto de Alencar Castello Branco, and Oliveiros S. Ferreira:

The era of charismatic leaders surrounded by a romantic aura is giving way to technocracy.[1]

Movements organized to achieve national salvation disgrace the national political power with fraudulent legality or legalistic farce in a phase of personality cults and oppression. Almost always, in order to act, salvation is aided by a symbolic man, a providential man, or a strong man. Emergencies create their own solution. National political power is the immediate end, and national power the instrument of authoritarianism.

Afterwards it is seen that the symbolic man does not live up to his role in an undertaking that carries the nation to disgrace, poverty, and submission; that the providential man is only providential for his immediate group, and by the evils that enslaved his people he cannot help but receive the malediction of his own Providence; and the strong man only serves to weaken the institutions and his own nation, transforming the national power into a bastion of pressure and violence over his fearful subjects.[2]

The charismatic leaders are finished, in spite of sympathy gained from liberal democratic quixotism mingled with pure charismatic authoritarianism as embodied in the former governor of Guanabara.[3] Logic tells us that he is the last representative of Brazilian political underdevelopment. This means that from now on the state will cease being a merry and liberal school in which the students come at a well-understood time, the teacher recites the lesson that he had learned the evening before, and everybody is promoted and receives a salary increase every December. All this signifies also that the personality of the leaders henceforth will contain only that minimum (summarily important, however) that is allowed by the structures and that it will be the organizations that will have the responsibility of mending public affairs.[4]

THE NEW ORDER & STRUCTURAL DEPENDENCE

Any ruler can refuse to accept the fundamental laws of social relations and history, but no one can govern against those laws. For this reason the new mode of leadership does not and can not win public option. It is very difficult for a collective group to move resolutely as a whole without an ideology in whose establishments and transformation it participated. The economic groups and social classes, or the masses, need to identify in some manner with the dominant ideology — if not, the separation between the rulers and the ruled will increase. In this sense, if it is true that the rulers since 1964 are attempting to reintegrate economic and political powers, then it is also true that the government and the people are dissociating themselves on a progressive scale. The people feel ruled but they do not feel that they are participating in the government. The power is unilaterally structured.

The businessmen were summoned to understand and adopt the new organizational patterns of the economic system and the political leadership. According to some official and unofficial ideologies, they were ready to adjust with efficacy to the requirements of the new mode of economic and political organization. In the words of Roberto de Abreu Sodré (elected by the State Assembly in 1966 as governor of the state of São Paulo) and Oliveiros S. Ferreira, the hegemony of military power over civil power will persist as long as the dominant class is not interested in assuming the reins of government directly.

If the civilians are absorbed in their own private business and have forgotten their duty toward their country, is it unusual that the military have taken their places even in the organization of civil society?

Either the businessmen understand their true role in the challenging times of today, adapting themselves to the mentality of this

184

new era, to new social and political conditions, to the new demands of the economy in the second half of the twentieth century, in order that "human necessities prevail over the mechanical equilibrium to which man almost entirely had been banished," in the judicious observation of François Perroux; or the businessmen proceed resolutely, cooperating in building civil order, intervening in political struggles, involving themselves personally, and assuming the risks arising from their actions without allowing themselves to be monopolized by their private affairs. This is their duty. If not, they must regret that others are acting without their dynamism and are incapable of understanding the irreplaceable mission of private economy. Thus, they will have created their own death sentence, and the only thing left for them to do is wait passively for the ever more brutal state invasion of economic life to the point of total state ownership.[5]

Military power will be able to be substituted only when the civil power is able to place its project in an organized fashion against the actual governmental action. And by a project I mean exactly that which allowed the Sorbonne to stay in authority and introduce a fellowship bridge to the young Turks — the most refined vision possible of the rationality of the system of production; the notion of social and economic demands imposed by this rationale when in confrontation with Brazilian society, history, and geography; the clear vision of natural resources possible for exploration and human resources available; the capacity to transform the vision of these demands to that which is purely theoretical, into a normative juridical system which organizes completely the society, keeping in mind the final objectives to be reached.[6]

Moreover, increased participation of businessmen and business groups in policy decisions and in the exercise of power itself already had been recommended and put into practice in previous years. The Institute for Research and Studies in the Social Sciences (IPES) and the Brazilian Institute for Democratic Action (IBAD) put this participation into concrete form. To the extent that growing dissociation is seen between political power and economic power in populist democracy, the businessmen are moved into action by their own means within or outside of political parties. In 1962 the development rate per capita fell by 0.5 percent and in 1963 it went to less than 1 percent. Parallel to this the businessmen were engaged seriously in political power. These relations appear clearly in the following quotations.

The growth rate of the Brazilian economy continued to decline in 1963. Estimates indicate an increment of only 2 percent against 3.7 percent in 1962 and 7.7 percent in 1961. In terms per capita in the last year (1963) the standard of living of the Brazilian population declined 1 percent.[7]

We fully agree that the producers participate in an active and decisive manner in the political life of the country, whether in electing their representatives for diverse federal and state government organs or by means of public opinion campaigns. We believe that the businessmen of Brazil have seen this necessity and already have taken the first moves to coordinate forces in this direction by the organization of various entities.[8]

In my mind the producers, as part of the national elite, can and must participate actively and manifestly in the political life of the nation. This participation must be that of permanent enlightening of public opinion for the virtues of our system of living. Our role is that of demonstrating to the people that democracy offers, in addition to guarantees of freedom, solutions for all our great problems. Thus if democratic political concepts are carried to the economic and social field, we discover that the road to progress is also the road to social justice.[9]

In this manner economics and politics meet again in intent and later in business. The recommendation of ideologists is equal to the demands of the more active sectors of the dominant class. Actually the Coup d'Etat of 1964 was one of the results of the political redefinition on the part of the more enlightened sectors of the dominant class together with military groups supported by the geopolitical doctrine of "Western civilization." This redefinition was dealing with a barrier against populist democracy and was seeking to restore the domination and appropriation structures that had been partially dissociated during the Vargas period.[10]

The creation of the Permanent Group for Industrial Mobilization in April, 1964, was an important aspect in the evolution of the ties between political and economic power, on the one hand, and military power, on the other hand. According to the businessmen who participated in the official opening meeting of this organ:

> The establishment of the Permanent Group for Industrial Mobilization, created at such an opportune time, is the continuation of the collaboration seen over the years between the producing classes and the armed forces, whether in periods of military action or in the normal life of our country.[11]

> The vivid experience of the first days [when the troops moved in to overthrow Goulart] showed the imperative necessity of industries to recognize the minimum requirements of the military and the latter to know with whom they can rely upon in industry. The armed forces employ equipment that is outside our industrial patterns and we do not know the requirements for material, equipment, and arms for the armed forces. It was essential to create a group of a permanent character that would do what we sought, civil and military, to act in time of danger. For this reason the Permanent Group for Industrial Mobilization will try to achieve the interlinking of industrial standards with the needs of the armed forces. It will give incentive to industrial research in the military field. It will reconcile industry to the manufacture of equipment, machines, and accessories for the armed forces. It will designate

the firms that are best adapted to execute the service or manufacture of military equipment. It will advise and recommend the adoption of standards for items which could be used in an emergency to benefit national security, giving the armed forces the result to the principal equation of modern warfare: Where to obtain material? When to obtain material? How to receive the necessary material? [12]

In this manner a new stage of institutionalizing the industrial-military complex was initiated in Brazil. Thus the domination system widened its scope, creating new conditions for the exercise of power. In this context let us insert the reflections of Oliveiros S. Ferreira on national greatness.

The conscience of a Great Power is not created if the power elite are not disposed to assume completely the implicit risks in the policy of greatness and, more specifically, if they do not agree to pay the price of the sacrifices that this policy imposes on the scale of individual consumption. . . .

Next to the permanent, well-equipped, and highly mobile combat army there exists another whose function will be, as General Góes Monteiro said, "to organize the shapeless masses with patriotic energy." [13]

Naturally the proletariat is the necessary counterpart to these ideological technical and governing worries. Therefore it is suggested that the workers in general accept the "new laborism," that is, a new image for their class interests to harmonize with the interests of other classes. The Minister of Planning and Economic Coordination, Roberto Campos, reveals a special preoccupation with this question.

Position of the Salaried Workers: The allotment of domestic income, using as a base the joint salaries, wages, profits, interests, rents, etc., in 1960 (which is the last year for which statistics are available), reveals that worker-sharing of remuneration in the internal income of the urban sector (estimated at 64.9 percent) is one of the highest in the international scene, surpassing that of various developed nations such as France, Germany, Italy, Switzerland, Belgium, Holland, Denmark, Austria, Australia, Japan, and New Zealand. There are few countries that are like the United States, England, Sweden, and Norway, where the percentage of internal income absorbed by the salaried workers exceeds that seen in Brazil in 1960.

The Laborite Illusion: On the other hand, and according to the following data, actual salaries have grown considerably up to 1959, tending, however, to decline from then on, especially in the last two years. The most important evidence of this (for lack of other more conclusive data) is furnished by variations in the minimum salary.

Paradoxically, however, it was precisely during the period in which laborism dominated the national scene that the workers suffered most in terms of actual acquisitive power because inflation canceled the massive nominal salary readjustments and the drop of the growth rate of the country occasioned the reduction in employment opportunities. In a parallel fashion it aggravated inequality between the salaried classes, promoting those with greater talent for political pressure, although not always the most productive, in detriment to the large mass of workers.[14]

The habitual process of salary revision in proportion greater or equal to the increase in cost of living is incompatible with the objectives of lowering inflation with development.[15]

Nothing is more urgent than to reconsider the role of laborism on the national scene, whether through its dynamic potentialities or through the high degree of intoxication to which it was exposed in the past. By being paternalistic since the Vargas era, laborism became unauthentic; by being unrealistic it became demagogic.

The first sin of past laborism was the obsessive preoccupation with massively high salaries. These were far beyond the productivity and growth increment possible from production. The natural result of this illusion was acceleration of the inflationary process.

The second sin of past laborism was its disinterest in other aspects of the workers' struggle, basically more significant than simply salary revision. Little did it cogitate on the opportunities for education and homeownership, including the purging and improvement of costly and inefficient social assistance and welfare services.

The third sin of past laborism was in the creation of a union-boss aristocracy. By means of an unusual bargain, some politically powerful classes, such as seamen, dock and railway workers, gained salary benefits much more rapidly than other sections of the working class who were politically less influential.

If in some cases, such as that of metallurgists and workers in the chemical industry, the salary increase reflected better training and productivity, in other cases the salary increase was based on simple political motivation while productivity decreased. The unions ceased being instruments for advancing workers in order to be transformed into vehicles of partisan politics.

The fourth sin of past laborism resided in relative indifference to investment level and, therefore, new employment opportunities.

This attitude is so egotistical as to be cruel. In planning salary levels not tied to productivity and possible revenue from services, the skilled and unskilled workers in transportation ended by decreasing government investment capacity and, therefore, its capacity to create productive employment for future generations.

Similarly, in applying pressure for unrealistic salary increases in the private sector they forced business to face the dilemma of rapidly canceling the salary increment by inflationary price rises or by reducing investment level, thereby canceling new job possibilities. In this way those already employed had the illusion of increased remuneration while condemning to unemployment or underemployment the future generations pouring into the labor market.

The fifth and gravest sin of past laborism resided in the dissolution of moral standards. With a terrible vengeance against indiscriminate accusations of Marx on the predatory spirit of capitalism exploiting surplus values, worker bossism exploited egotistically the more unprotected elements of the working class.[16]

This is the new image of laborism in opposition to a supposed dispersion of the rule of the masses in effect until 1964. Based on this interpretation of class relations regarding product sharing, the rulers formulate new directives of social policy. The main points of workers' policy inaugurated after the vic-tory over populist democracy are the following:

a) To eliminate participation by the salaried workers, par-ticularly the proletariat, in political decisions in general. To eliminate or reduce considerably union interference in federal, state, and municipal political events.

b) To control (or cancel) the capacity of bourgeois groups opposed to the economic policy initiated in 1964 (open and full association with international capital and foreign organi-zations) who support the salaried workers or function as their spokesman. Actually this was meant to weaken the political base of nationalistic sectors identified with the nationalist model for development.

c) Consequently, to restore the control of the dominant class over the conduct of the fundamental factor of production, manipulating the relative cost of labor and its productive effectiveness as completely as possible. For this reason the principle of job stability (after ten years of employment with the company) was changed to unemployment insurance, thus freeing the company from a fixed and permanent responsibility. In other words, salary confiscation by means of rigid and centralized control of workers' politics and union movements was restored.

d) In short, to liquidate the rule of the masses as a technique for sustaining political power and as the essential manifestation of people's politics. With this goal the strike laws were altered rigorously, controlling the possibilities of their utilization as an economic or political claims technique.

THE NEW ORDER & STRUCTURAL DEPENDENCE

As we can see, class relations were reformulated juridically and politically in terms that were clear enough and different from the definition before 1964. The legislative modifications over political parties, unionization, strikes, social welfare, etc., reveal the basic structure of the new image of laborism in Brazil.

There has not been the necessary uniformity in verification and application of indices for the reconstitution of average actual salary in the last twenty-four months based on the salary policy followed by the government as an instrument to combat inflation; . . . this lack of uniformity results in granting different percentages of salary increase even within the same professional category; . . . the lack of uniformity and precision in the ascertainment of indices and divergent criteria in the application of the legislation in force has contributed frequently to granting salary increases that conflicted with the general orientation of the government's financial and economic policy; . . . social peace, a fundamental requisite for national security, demands an equitable salary policy for the working class within itself, without discriminatory treatment in benefit or detriment to any professional category.[17]

The strike will be proclaimed illegal (1) if it is not within the period and conditions established by this law; (2) if it has for an objective claims judged invalid by the Labor Court in a definite decision handed down less than a year ago; (3) if caused by political, partisan, religious, or social motives with support or solidarity of groups without any claim that directly or legitimately interests the said professional category; (4) if it has as a goal to alter a constant in the union agreement, a collective labor convention, or a normative decision of the Labor Court in force, unless the fundamentals which they support have been modified substantially.[18]

This new image of laborism is not concerned with being in favor of or against demagoguery and charismatic leaders. It deals with understanding its conditions of existence, its historic and cultural roots. Particularly necessary is a recognition of the divergent currents of option in leaders and organizations. It is necessary to admit the multiplicity of political currents and the divergency of class interests upon which are based distinct developmental models. If this is not done, political power evolves in a monolithic form, making the relations of domination and the modalities of worker-sharing in the national product concrete.

Actually there are significant ties and correspondences between the doctrine of interdependence and the doctrine of reversal of expectations, as in domestic and foreign policy. These two doctrines are essentially manifestations of the basic model for modernizing Brazilian society, that is, consolidation of the status quo in authoritarian terms. They are destined to achieve the reintegration of political and economic power, consolidating the hegemony of the dominant class.

We can no longer be indifferent to the fortunes of our neighbors, nor stand with crossed arms in face of the violence of foreign aggression through internal forces. Every subversive front is a threat to our rear guard and jeopardizes the freedom of all people. Today it is in the Caribbean [a reference to the presence of Brazilian troops in the Dominican Republic, having been called by the OAS]. And nobody doubts that having succeeded in establishing itself there, it will not delay in choosing and attacking a new victim. . . .

Nevertheless, in the fight that is placed upon us to save democracy, this comprehension in reference to our international duties and needs is not sufficient. It is as important, or more so, that democracy on the home front not be compromised by those who, instead of seeking to fulfill their special or normal missions, plan in reality to transform themselves into an autonomous force, pernicious and inadmissible in attaining the objectives of the revolution. It does not matter that they are enthused with patriotic intentions, since the truth is that instead of helping to strengthen and consolidate the regime, they contribute toward opening rifts in areas which must be the pillars of our democracy. In place of aid they divert their strength, conveying lack of confidence where it would be better to bring greater confidence in the regime. All this certainly occurs because they have forgotten that the justice or the perfection that they wish flows inevitably from a system, and never from isolated impulses that divide when they should unite.

I must, however, affirm that the government does not submit to any detour whatsoever in authority. This is not merely its duty, but the public does not want agitation, whether from the seat of government or from those who are malcontent for not having the gratification of power. The people want juridical order, they want elections, they want the legitimate exercise of authority by rulers, they want to sense the cohesive support of the armed forces for the rapid rise of the country. This is the orientation followed resolutely by the government within its obligations and prerogatives.[19]

Here we have the background for understanding the extinction of the political parties that had existed up to 1964, and for the divesting of technicians, politicians, workers, intellectuals, military men, and students of their political rights for ten years. At the core of the fight against charismatic leaders and demagogues is the concept and exercise of authoritarian power. In the name of organization and effectiveness a dictatorship was established.[20] Hypertrophy of executive power is the essence of the economic policy adopted after April 1, 1964. In addition, there is the necessity for the destruction of populist democracy. A vast mobilization of political and ideological resources is required when one plans to eliminate values and patterns, techniques and ambitions, created in decades of struggling and accumulated in increasing quantity by the Brazilian people.

In this sense the Institutional Acts, the new Constitution

passed by the legislature in 1967, university reform, and control of union and student organizations are interlinked events. They are intended to reunite politics and economics and set them in a new direction. They are designed to overthrow the nationalist model of development as a power and as the economic policy structure.

CHAPTER 13

CONCLUSIONS

Throughout this study I have tried to reconstruct the events, relations, and political tendencies of Brazil as a dynamic system. As much as possible I have described what has occurred at the climaxes in Brazilian politico-economic development and at the same time pointed out what could have occurred. I tried to reproduce the active events as well as those that were roughly drafted, remaining scarcely potentialities. In such terms the preceding chapters are an effort to reconstruct the conditions, the possibilities, and the limits surrounding the development of Brazilian politico-economic systems.

With this in mind the present analysis dwells especially on the crises, tensions, and uncertainties that appeared in these decades. I wanted to follow the political and economic processes against the background of the principal and secondary controversies. Since I wanted to interpret Brazilian society beginning with the transformations and crises that occurred in political and economic structures, I examined first the list of structural breaks in recent decades. The successions and the external and internal interrelationships in these ruptures were recorded. Simultaneously the relations between political and economic processes were analyzed, considering changes in terms of the worldwide social structure.

Consequently the examination of events brought us to the

problem of imperialism, as well as to that of the role of the Brazilian bourgeoisie. Class relationships appear as they actually were, that is, either obscure or clear, antagonistic or accommodating. Populist democracy in its different modalities (getulismo, workers' movements, leftism, etc.) has been characterized and interpreted in the social and economic context in which it actually arose. The formation, climax, and collapse of the rule of the masses, which is also known as populist democracy, was reconstructed. Let us look at a synthesis of this historical picture in light of significant present events.

Brazilian populist democracy arose under Vargas and politicians associated with him. Beginning in 1930 this new political movement was gradually organized. Alongside concrete measures, its ideology and jargon were developed. While the rulers were taking care of some of the demands of the urban proletariat, populist institutions and symbols developed simultaneously. Slowly the labor market was standardized in the expanding urban industrial milieu and at the same time the masses came to play real, but still secondary, political roles. Thus it can be asserted that the entry of the masses into the power structure was justified through the intermediacy of popular movements. Initially this popular front was exclusively getulista. Afterwards it acquired other connotations and other denominations. Borghismo, queremismo, juscelinismo, janguismo, and labor movements are some of the varieties of Brazilian populist democracy. In addition, the rule of the masses, specific for one stage in the socioeconomic and political transformations in Brazil, was a political movement before it was a political party. It corresponded to a fundamental part of the political manifestations that occurred in a determined phase of transformations in the industrial sector and, on a lesser scale,

CONCLUSIONS

in the agrarian sector. In addition, it was dynamically related to the urbanization and development of the tertiary sector of Brazilian economy. It was related even more to mass consumption, as well as to the appearance of mass culture. To sum up, Brazilian populist democracy was a political form adopted by mass society in the country.

We can see that the rule of the masses was bourgeois and leftist. Sometimes its leaders were men who originated from the people, or even leftist groups or parties. Other times its leaders were actually from the bourgeoisie. In the majority of cases the bourgeois leaders dominated the populist scene, controlling the bureaucratic mechanism of parties and the organizations bound to the rule of the masses. In general they were the most successful demagogues in controlling the masses. Some of them reached the category of charismatic personalities.

Populist democracy collapsed after the government of Juscelino Kubitschek. The truth is that it was a political movement in a permanent state of crisis. In a bourgeois society it is always extremely difficult to justify the political participation of the working masses. The entrenched holders of political power and the dominant economic groups invariably had to face two sorts of pressure in their relationship to, and control of, the masses. On the one hand, the more conservative and reactionary sections of Brazilian society always protested violently against engaging the masses politically. They saw in this a warning for the destruction of bourgeois power and its external bonds. In addition, these same sectors protested and fought against the rule of the masses because they understood that the masses were being used to strengthen the bargaining capacity (internal and external) of the industrial bourgeoisie in the Brazilian market. On the other hand, the bourgeoisie that was itself compromised by populist tendencies always was uncertain and divided in the limits of its interplay with the masses. The participation of the workers in urban and industrial centers in election campaigns (local, state, and national), in nationalistic movements, in anti-imperialistic fights, and in debates for basic institutional reforms favored and developed the training of the salaried workers in politics. For these reasons populist democracy was punctuated by crises. The deposition and suicide of Vargas in 1954 symbolized, above all, the conjunction of pressures and doubts that characterized the history of the Brazilian popular front.

At all times the Left was related, directly and indirectly, to populist democracy. The majority and even the more radical sectors believed that to infiltrate the movements of the masses was a viable technique of leftist political action. At the time that the leftist political groups and parties were organizing themselves independently, they were infiltrating and allying themselves with populist movements, campaigns, parties, and leaders. They wished to conquer the masses by this means. In the majority of cases, however, they transformed themselves into populists, enveloping themselves with populist techniques, jargon, and interpretations. In any case, the bond between the Left and populist democracy was one more source for tension and conflict and another reason why the movement was in a state of permanent crisis.

With this we begin to understand the reasons for the collapse of the popular front in 1964. While in its internal organization populist democracy is a system of antagonisms, as a policy for class alliances it is a policy for the alliance of opposites. At the same time, its position politically in a capitalistic society created

CONCLUSIONS

new conditions for crisis. During times of normalcy the alliance always worked to some degree, but during critical occasions the antagonisms showed their heads.

Let us look at the conditions that bred the crisis and collapse of populist democracy. In the first place, it is important to mention that in 1962 the long period of economic expansion in Brazil came to a close. In 1963 an economic crisis was in full swing, and inflation stopped being a technique for forced savings. The profit inflation became a cost inflation, that is, the inflationary spiral acquired pathological connotations. Capitalistic reproduction began to enter a neutral position.

Because of the acceleration of the inflationary process, the masses came to demand salary increases more and more frequently. Workers began an almost uninterrupted fight to avoid the excessive lowering of the purchasing power of their salaries. The salary protests and strikes were manifestations of the workers' struggle against the confiscation of their salaries due to inflation. Because of this the workers developed union organizations, strengthened their confederations, and broadened their relations with the populist parties and the Left.

The truth is that the rule of the masses was gaining fast at a time when the political power of the bourgeoisie was weakening. Engagement with the masses, conceived by a sector of the bourgeoisie itself, was no longer endurable for the dominant class. Risks were growing, and populist democracy was beginning to extend to the agrarian society. Peasant leagues and the rural unions were multiplying and gaining force through the PTB, the PC, and the Catholic Church in accordance with populist techniques. The struggle for agrarian reform itself functioned as a means to augment the force of the rural workers' movement.

CONCLUSIONS

Faced with this situation the agrarian, industrial, commercial, and financial bourgeoisie united. They understood that the crisis brought with it various possibilities for the resolution of the impasse. On the one hand, the conditions for an actual revolutionary solution, that is, for a socialist revolution, were increasing. In conjunction with the political crisis the economic crisis became more acute. Economic and political tensions were being joined, thereby weakening the bourgeois power. Besides this a rapid and broad politicizing of the salaried working masses was taking place, as well as an increase in the political participation of rural workers.

On the other hand, bourgeois and middle-class leaders dedicated to a project for national capitalism could see how to profit by the situation. Nationalism had prepared the country for a redefinition of relations with the United States. The independent foreign policy continued to show many indications in this direction. The counterpart of an independent foreign policy was necessarily national capitalism, that is, a capitalistic system regulated by active national decision-making centers. This alternative was implicit in the Plano Trienal that João Goulart never succeeded in implementing.

The majority of foreign and Brazilian bourgeois sectors — agrarian, industrial, commercial, and financial — not only understood the situation but acted with the greatest speed. Of all the choices that developed during the critical period of populist democracy, what was imposed was a bourgeois dictatorship. It was imposed with the ostensible approval of the United States government. Under military protection the doctrine of interdependence was installed with political, economic, military, and cultural orientations.

Based upon a conception that was out of phase with world

CONCLUSIONS

geopolitical systems, a dictatorship completely obligated to the United States was put into practice by the revolutionaries of 1964. Exactly when the hegemony of Washington and Moscow was at a crisis, those who held power in Brazil began to change and improve the dependent relation of Brazil on the United States. In the middle of the second phase of the cold war, the Brazilian rulers were using criteria developed in the first phase. Moreover, anachronism is one of the essential characteristics of the structural dependence that defines underdevelopment.

In the name of the principles of interdependence, what has occurred since 1964 has been a total reformulation of Brazil's foreign dependency. In political relations as in economic, in military relations as in cultural, there has occurred or is occurring a redefinition. Consequently the structural dependency which had characterized the history of Brazilian society is deepening even more. I maintain, in agreement with the intimation of Helio Jaguaribe, that a colonial-fascist regime was inaugurated in Brazil in 1964, a regime defined by submission to the politico-military principles of a geopolitical system developed according to Washington's perspective in the first phase of the cold war.

In 1964 a political regime influenced by structural dependency came into power, as emphasized earlier. In particular, during Kubitschek's administration economic dependence became greater. Previously a redefinition of the political functions of the armed forces had been initiated and the principle of national defense gradually was replaced by the principle of national security. It is convenient to remember here that the Brazilian military forces that fought in Europe in World War II were under the command of the American military forces. Beginning with this period there developed an increasingly intense exchange between the two military organizations. At the same time, on the political level the redefinition of foreign dependency was stimulated by progress in the accelerated political participation of the masses. The American rulers always confronted getulismo and some of its variants with reserve or hostility. Consequently all progress in mass movements in Brazil was acted upon as an element for alarm on the part of conservative and reactionary groups. In this context notions of union dictatorship and revolutionary war are applied to nourish ideologically the movement for a coup d'état.

The government inaugurated in 1964 returned to two fundamental objectives. It has reenforced and broadened the foreign bonds of dependence under the aegis of "doctrine of interdependence." It has developed an ideological and political campaign opposing all manifestations of the rule of the masses. It seeks to destroy the organizations, techniques, and ideologies created during the operation of populist democracy. The actions of the government are found to eliminate simultaneously the possibilities of socialism as well as the possibilities of a nationalistic capitalism. In the name of purification (or modernization) of the Brazilian politico-economic system, a fascist culture is being created. Victims of the Manichaeanism inherent in its conception of political process, the rulers, and the economic groups that they serve, are building fascist institutions, symbols, and attitudes. This is the price that the Brazilian people are paying for open militarization of political power. Moreover, the tendency toward fascism is another characteristic essential to structural dependency.

Since 1964 the Right has been becoming more radical on the Brazilian political scene. The militarization of political power is only a symptom of this process. The dictatorship of the bourgeoisie has been developed and consolidated in the name of an arbitrary conception of social stability and internal security. In the midst of a stagnated economy, a political stagnation is evolving as well. Even more than this, the rulers put into practice a conception of power that produces political decadence. This decadence does not necessarily touch the entire Brazilian society. It reaches first the bourgeois sectors themselves and secondly their foundation in the middle class, which obviously creates new conditions for revolution. At the base of the stability and security policy is the divorce between the established power and the salaried masses. Political power is arbitrarily exercised by a group obligated to the most powerful sectors of the dominant class — obligated in its economic interests as well as in its ideology. It is that ideology that inspires the convenient geopolitical principles in the interests of multinational corporations.

In opposing the probable or imaginary possibilities for the formation of a nationalistic capitalism, the rulers are sowing fresh seeds for socialism. Simultaneously, by opposing in a violent manner any and all manifestations of a really free and independent union or party life, they are creating further political conditions indispensable for revolutionary activity. As prisoners of economic and political interests of the dominant class, particularly those organized in the area of multinational corporations, they have not succeeded in solving the most important problems of Brazilian society. For these reasons, labor, rural, and university problems, among others, are confronted as problems related to sociopolitical stability or the conveniences of internal security. The traditional relations of foreign dependency are breeding new institutions and a bigger idea factory. As a general result, the heart of the matter is obscured or remains on a secondary level.

The relations between social classes thus acquire ever more significant outlines. As long as mass movements in the rural and urban proletariat are suffocated, more propitious conditions are created for the class struggle. Populist democracy will have been only one stage in the history of the relations between social classes. In this sense it may be said that while populist democracy terminates in the class struggle, fascist dictatorship may terminate in the socialist society.

NOTES

CHAPTER 2

Tensions and Conflicts

1. Alan K. Manchester, *British Preeminence in Brazil, Its Rise and Decline: A Study in European Expansion* (Chapel Hill, University of North Carolina Press, 1933), pp. 329-36.
2. Jordan Young, "Military Aspects of the 1930 Brazilian Revolution," *Hispanic American Historical Review*, XLIV, No. 2 (May, 1964), 193.

CHAPTER 3

Phases of Industrialization

1. Celso Furtado, *Formação Econômica do Brasil* (Rio de Janeiro, Editôra Fundo de Cultura, 1959), pp. 234-35.
2. Raul Prebisch, *Hacia una Dinámica del Desarrollo Latinoamericano* (Mexico, Fondo de Cultura Económica, 1963), pp. x-xi.
3. For the concept of the growing presence of foreign capital in public and private finances in Brazil see J. Pandiá Calógeras, *A Política Monetária do Brasil* (São Paulo, Companhia Editôra Nacional, 1960; 1st edition in French, 1910); Carlos Inglez de Souza, *A Anarchia Monetária e suas Consequências* (São Paulo, Editôra Monteiro Lobato, 1924).
4. Juscelino Kubitschek de Oliveira, *Mensagem ao Congresso Nacional* (Rio de Janeiro, 1957), pp. 246-48.
5. Juscelino Kubitschek de Oliveira, *Mensagem ao Congresso Nacional* (Rio de Janeiro, 1959), pp. 100-1.
6. Octavio Ianni, *Estado e Capitalismo* (Rio de Janeiro, Editôra Civilização Brasileira, 1965), pp. 43 and 47.

CHAPTER 4

Agrarian Development

1. Pei-kang Chang, *Agricultura e Industrialización*, trans. Juan F.

NOTES: AGRARIAN DEVELOPMENT

Noyola and Edmundo Flores (Mexico, Fondo de Cultura Económica, 1951), p. 284.

2. *Revista Brasileira de Economia*, Ano 17, No. 1 (Rio de Janeiro, March, 1963), p. 15; Instituto Brasileiro de Geografia e Estatística (IBGE), *Anuario Estatístico do Brasil* (Rio de Janeiro, IBGE, 1965), p. 33.

3. José Francisco de Camargo, *Exodo Rural no Brasil*, Bulletin No. 1 (Faculty of Economics and Administration, University of São Paulo, 1957).

4. Paulo Schilling, *Trigo* (Rio de Janeiro, ISEB, 1959), pp. 23-24, 26-27. See also his *Crise Econômica no Rio Grande do Sul* (Pôrto Alegre, Difusão de Cultura Técnica, 1961).

5. Rui Miller Paiva and William H. Nichols, "Estágio do Desenvolvimento Técnico da Agricultura Brasileira," *Revista Brasileira de Economia*, Ano 19, No. 3 (Rio de Janeiro, 1965), pp. 27-63; quotation from p. 61.

6. Chang, *Agricultura e Industrialización*, pp. 280-81.

7. Celso Furtado, *A Operação Nordeste* (Rio de Janeiro, ISEB, 1959), pp. 57-60.

CHAPTER 5

Getulismo

1. *Consolidação das Leis do Trabalho,* approved by Decree Law No. 5,452 of May 1, 1943, arts. 578-95.

2. Octavio Ianni, *Estado e Capitalismo* (Rio de Janeiro, Editôra Civilização Brasileira, 1965), p. 159.

3. Orlando M. Carvalho, *Ensaios de Sociologia Eleitoral* (Belo Horizonte, Edição RBEP, 1958), p. 104.

4. Getúlio Vargas, *Mensagem ao Congresso Nacional* (Rio de Janeiro, 1951), p. 7.

5. Jânio Quadros, *Mensagem ao Congresso Nacional* (Brasília, 1961), pp. 82-83.

6. "Vargas Teria Revelado à Alemanha em 1940 o seu Propósito de Manter a Neutralidade," *Fôlha da Manhã* (São Paulo), June 1, 1956.

7. Vargas, *Mensagem ao Congresso Nacional*, p. 19.

8. Getúlio Vargas, "Carta Testamento," printed in Nelson Werneck Sodré, *Formacão Histórica do Brasil* (São Paulo, Editôra Brasiliense, 1962), pp. 412-13.

9. Quadros, *Mensagem ao Congresso Nacional*, pp. 84-85.

10. San Tiago Dantas, *Política Externa Independente* (Rio de Janeiro, Editôra Civilização Brasileira, 1962), pp. 17-18.

11. João Goulart, *Desenvolvimento e Independência* (Brasília, Serviço Gráfico do Instituto Brasileiro de Geografia e Estatística, 1962), pp. 88-89 and 128.

CHAPTER 6

Rule of the Masses in the Rural Zones

1. *Contrato de Parceira Agrícola*, printed in "Os Arrendatários Esperam a Intervenção do Govêrno," article in *O Estado de São Paulo*, August 6, 1960, p. 10.

2. "Solução Judicial Para os Arrendamentos de Terra na Zona de Santa Fé do Sul," article in *O Estado de São Paulo*, August 3, 1960, p. 12. More on the proletarianization of the rural worker in São Paulo can be found in Moisés Vinhas, *Operários e Camponeses na Revolução Brasileira* (São Paulo, Editôra Fulgor, 1963).

3. Celso Furtado, *Dialética do Desenvolvimento* (Rio de Janeiro, Editôra Fundo de Cultura, 1964), pp. 143-45.

4. Miguel Arraes, *Palavra de Arraes* (Rio de Janeiro, Editôra Civilização Brasileira, 1965), pp. 101-3.

5. "Padre Melo: Nao Há Communismo no NE, mas Insatisfação," *O Estado de São Paulo*, May 5, 1962, p. 40.

6. "Declaração de Belo Horizonte," presented at the closing of the First National Congress of Laborers and Agricultural Workers, Belo Horizonte, November 17, 1961. Printed in Francisco Julião, *Que São as Ligas Camponesas* (Rio de Janeiro, Editôra Civilização Brasileira, 1962), pp. 84-85.

NOTES: THE LEFT AND THE MASSES

CHAPTER 7

The Left and the Masses

1. Getúlio Vargas, *As Diretrizes da Nova Política do Brasil* (Rio de Janeiro, José Olympio Editôra, 1942), pp. 209-10, 215, and 218-20. This is an anthology of speeches and statements by Vargas.

2. Getúlio Vargas, *A Política Trabalhista no Brasil* (Rio de Janeiro, José Olympio Editôra, 1950), pp. 188-89.

3. Juscelino Kubitschek de Oliveira, *Mensagem ao Congresso National* (Rio de Janeiro, 1960), pp. 131 and 132-33.

4. João Goulart, *Mensagem ao Congresso Nacional* (Brasília, 1963), pp. 137 and 139.

5. João Goulart, *Mensagem ao Congresso Nacional* (Brasília, 1964, pp. 177-78.

6. Translator's note: Leonel Brizolla is Goulart's brother-in-law and was governor of the state of Rio Grande do Sul.

7. On this subject see "Perspectivas da Esquerda," by Gabriel Cohn, and "Política de Masses," by Francisco C. Weffort, in *Política e Revolução Social no Brasil,* by O. Ianni, P. Singer, G. Cohn, and F. C. Weffort (Rio de Janeiro, Editôra Civilização Brasileira, 1965).

8. Leôncio Martins Rodrigues, *Conflito Industrial e Sindicalismo no Brasil* (São Paulo, Difusão Européia do Livro, 1966), p. 57.

9. Program printed in Jorge Miglioli, *Como São Feitas as Greves no Brasil* (Rio de Janeiro, Editôra Civilização Brasileira, 1963), pp. 117-18.

10. "O Movimento Operário e a Política Sindical dos Comunistas," document printed as an appendix in Jover Telles, *O Movimento Sindical no Brasil* (Rio de Janeiro, Editorial Vitória, 1962), pp. 285-301; quotation from pp. 291-92.

11. *Resolução Política da Convençã Nacional dos Comunistas* (Rio de Janeiro, 1961), pp. 15-16.

12. *Política Operária,* Ano III, No. 5 (Rio de Janeiro, 1963), pp. 51-52 ("Pela União dos Marxistas Revolucionários").

13. *Política Operária,* Ano III, No. 6 (Rio de Janeiro, 1963), pp. 4-6.

NOTES: CONTRADICTIONS

14. *Movimento,* magazine of the National Students' Union (UNE), No. 12 (Rio de Janeiro, 1963), p. 24.

15. *Constituição,* National Students' Union (UNE) (Rio de Janeiro, 1963), art. 3.

16. Marialice Mencarini Foracchi, *O Estudante e a Transformação da Sociedade Brasileira* (São Paulo, Companhia Editôra Nacional, 1965), p. 294.

17. Caio Prado, Jr., *A Revolução Brasileira* (São Paulo, Editôra Brasiliense, 1966), pp. 33-34.

18. Antônio Gramsci, *Concepção Dialética da História,* trans. Carlos Nelson Coutinho (Rio de Janeiro, Editôra Civilização Brasileira, 1966), p. 23.

CHAPTER 8

Contradictions in the Nationalist Model

1. Fernando Pedreira, *Março 31 (Civis e Militares no Processo da Crise Brasileira)* (Rio de Janeiro, José Alvaro Editor, 1964), p. 168.

2. João Goulart, *Desenvolvimento e Independência* (speeches) (Brasília, Serviço Gráfico do IBGE, 1962), pp. 91-92.

3. San Tiago Dantas, *Idéias e Rumos para a Revolução Brasileira* (Rio de Janeiro, José Olympio Editôra, 1963), pp. 14-15. For more on the attempt to affirm an independent foreign policy see Jânio Quadros, "Brazil's New Foreign Policy," *Foreign Affairs,* XL, No. 1 (October, 1961), pp. 19-27.

4. Presidência da República, *Plano Trienal de Desenvolvimento Econômico e Social (1963-1965)* (synthesis) (Rio de Janeiro, Departamento da Imprensa Nacional, 1963), pp. 32-33. Attributed to Celso Furtado, then Minister Extraordinary of Planning.

5. Henry Rijken van Olst, "Desarrollo Económico y Cooperación en América Latina," appendix in Jan Tinbergen, *Hacia Una Economía Mundial,* trans. Anna M. Cabré (Barcelona, Ediciones de Occidente, 1965), pp. 213-26; quotation from p. 217.

6. Antônio Dias Leite, *Caminhos do Desenvolvimento: Contribução para un projeto brasileiro* (Rio de Janeiro, Zahar Editôres, 1966), p. 129.

7. Celso Furtado, *Dialética do Desenvolvimento* (Rio de Janeiro, Editôra Fundo de Cultura, 1964), pp. 120-21.

8. Ministério do Planejamento e Coordenção Econômica, *Programa de Ação Econômica do Govêrno, 1964-1966*, Documentos EPEA, No. 1 (Rio de Janeiro, November, 1964), p. 19.

CHAPTER 9

The Coup d'Etat

1. Francisco C. Weffort, "Raízes Sociais do Populismo em São Paulo," *Revista Civilização Brasileira*, Ano 1, No. 2 (Rio de Janeiro, 1965); Gláucio Ary Dillon Soares, "As Bases Ideológicas do Lacerdismo," *Revista Civilização Brasileira*, Ano 1, No. 4 (Rio de Janeiro, 1965).

2. "Memorial dos Coronéis," in Oliveiros S. Ferreira, *As Fôrças Armadas e o Desafio da Revolução* (Rio de Janeiro, Edições GRD, 1964), pp. 122-29; quotation from p. 127.

3. Oliveira Vianna, *O Ocaso do Império*, 2d ed. (São Paulo, Comp. Melhoramentos de São Paulo, n.d.), p. 131. This work was written in 1925.

4. General Juarez Távora, "O Petróleo do Brasil," Parlimentary Documents, *Petróleo*, II, 382. General J. C. Horta Barbosa, *ibid.*, p. 410.

5. Octavio Ianni, *Estado e Capitalismo* (Rio de Janeiro, Editôra Civilização Brasileira, 1965), pp. 240-41. However, the same active participation of the military already had been observed previously on the occasion of debates on the formation of the steel industry. The construction of the steel mill at Volta Redonda, begun in 1943, met with open interference by the military.

6. "Instrução Reservada do General Castelo Branco" (Confidential Instructions from General Castelo Branco), Army Chief of Staff to the generals and other officers of the Army General Staff and subordinate organizations. Printed in Alberto Dines, Antônio Callado, *et al.*, *Os Idos de Março* (Rio de Janeiro, José Alvaro Editor, 1964), pp. 392-93.

7. "Posição do Estado Maior das Fôrças Armadas Face aos

Recentes Acontecimentos Ocorridos no País" (Position of the General Staff of the Armed Forces in View of the Recent Events in the Country), confidential document delivered by General of the Army Pery Constant Bevilacqua, Armed Forces Chief of Staff, to the President of the Republic on March 31, 1964. Quoted in Bilac Pinto, *Guerra Revolucionária* (Rio de Janeiro, Forense, July, 1964), pp. 208-11.

8. "Ato Institucional," No. 1, April 9, 1964, in Mario Victor, *5 Anos que Abalaram o Brasil* (Rio de Janeiro, Editôra Civilização Brasileira, 1965), pp. 597-98.

9. Pinto, *Guerra Revolucionária*, p. 47. Consult also *A revolução de 31 de Março, 2° Aniversário, Colaboração do Exército* (Rio de Janeiro, Bibliotec do Exército, 1966), which combines the studies of Marshal Humbreto de Alencar Castello Branco, Marshal Arthur da Costa e Silva, José Américo de Almeida, Miguel Reale, and others. For a clarification of the action of political forces opposed to populist democracy and to nationalist development see Paulo Singer, "A Política das Classes Dominantes," in *Política e Revolução Social no Brasil*, by O. Ianni, P. Singer, G. Cohn, and F. C. Weffort (Rio de Janeiro, Editôra Civilização Brasileira, 1965).

10. Edwin Lieuwen, *U.S. Policy in Latin America: A Short History* (New York, Frederick A. Praeger, 1965), pp. 122-23. For more on the coup, see also the same author's *Generals vs. Presidents: Neomilitarism in Latin America* (New York, Frederick A. Praeger, 1965), esp. Chap. 4, "1964: Brazil," pp. 69-85.

11. General Golbery do Couto e Silva, *Aspectos Geopolíticos de Brasil* (Rio de Janeiro, Biblioteca do Exército, 1957), pp. 49-50.

12. Alan K. Manchester, *British Preeminence in Brazil, Its Rise and Decline: A Study in European Expansion* (Chapel Hill, University of North Carolina Press, 1933); J. F. Normano, *Evolução Econômica do Brasil*, 2d ed. (São Paulo, Companhia Editôra Nacional, 1945); J. F. Normano, *A Luta Pela América do Sul* (São Paulo, Editôra Atlas, 1944).

13. Lieuwen, *U.S. Policy in Latin America*, p. 111.

14. Thomas Mann, "Apoio dos Estados Unidos à Democracia na América Latina," *O Estado de São Paulo*, June 21, 1964, p. 15.

213

15. Herbert L. Matthews, "Understanding Latin America," in *The United States and Latin America* (The American Assembly, Columbia University, New York, December, 1959), pp. 1-2.

16. W. Feuerlein and E. Hannan, *Dólares en la América Latina* (Mexico, Fondo de Cultura Económica, 1944), p. 17.

17. *Ibid.*, p. 8.

18. "L'Alleanza Russia America," editorial in *L'Espresso* (Rome), December 5, 1965, Anno XI, No. 49, p. 1.

CHAPTER 10

The Structural Dependence

1. Antônio Dias Leite, *Caminhos do Desenvolvimento: Contribuição para um projeto brasileiro* (Rio de Janeiro, Zahar Editôres, 19666), p. 122. The same problem was focused upon simultaneously by Simon Kuznets, *Modern Economic Growth* (New Haven, Yale University Press, 1966), pp. 286-94, "Transnational Stock Knowledge."

2. J. F. Normano, *Evolução Económica do Brasil* (São Paulo, Companhia Editóra Nacional, 1945), p. 283. See also the same author's *A Luta Pela América do Sul* (São Paulo, Editôra Atlas, 1944).

3. Paolo Sylos Labini, *Oligopólio y Progresso Técnico* (Barcelona, Ediciones Oikos-Tau, 1965), p. 28. See also Paul A. Baran and Paul M. Sweezy, *Monopoly Capital: An Essay on the American Economic and Political Order* (New York, Monthly Review Press, 1966).

4. Corwin D. Edwards, "Contróle de Mercados e Preços," in *A Missão Cooke no Brasil* (Rio de Janeiro, Fundaçáo Getúlio Vargas, 1949), pp. 372-435; quotation from pp. 376-77.

5. Alberto Passos Guimarães, *Inflação e Monopólio no Brasil* (Rio de Janeiro, Editóra Civilização Brasileira, 1963), p. 64. Also consult *Desenvolvimento e Conjuntura*, Ano V, No. 5 (Rio de Janeiro, May, 1961), and *Quem Controla o Que* (3d edition of *O Capital Estrangeiro no Brasil*), edited by Robert Gongeard,

NOTES: THE STRUCTURAL DEPENDENCE

Benedito Ribeiro, Regina Lorch, and Elisabeth Banas (São Paulo, Editôra Banas S/A, 1961), 2 vols.

6. "Instrução No. 113" of the Superintendency of Money and Credit (SUMOC), January 17, 1955, printed in Aristóteles Moura, *Capitais Estrangeiros no Brasil* (São Paulo, Editôra Brasiliense, 1959), pp. 361-64; quotation from p. 361.

7. In announcing the merger of Vemag with Volkswagen in November, 1966, Lelio Piza Filho, president of Vemag, pointed out the following: "We associated with Massey-Ferguson to begin production of tractors and agricultural machinery; with Scania Vabis to produce trucks; and finally with the Auto Union we now produce via certificate No. 1 of GEIA the first Brazilian passenger vehicle. The association initially made with Auto Union and subsequently transferred to Volkswagen of Germany has just been broadened in the greater interest of our national economy." *Fôlha de São Paulo*, November 9, 1966, p. 11.

8. "Instrução 113 de SUMOC e Desnacionalização," editorial of *O Estado de São Paulo*, January 13, 1961.

9. Maurício Vinhas de Queiroz, "Os Grupos Multibilionários," *Revista do Instituto de Ciências Sociais*, II, No. 1 (Rio de Janeiro, 1965), 47-77; quotation from pp. 75-77. As the president of Vemag states regarding their association with Volkswagen: "Certain transactions flow from the groups involved in them, not only for their intrinsic value, but also for the repercussions which penetrate the very economic life of the country." *Fôlha de São Paulo*, November 11, 1966, p. 11.

10. Arthur M. Schlesinger, Jr., *A Thousand Days: John F. Kennedy in the White House* (Boston, Houghton Mifflin Co., 1965), p. 172.

11. *Ibid.*, p. 192.

12. Brookings Institution, *Major Problems of United States Foreign Policy, 1954* (Menasha, Wis., George Banta Publishing Company, 1954), pp. 338, 340-41.

13. Adolf A. Berle, *Latin America: Diplomacy and Reality* (New York, Harper & Row, for the Council on Foreign Relations, 1962), pp. 23-24.

14. "Morse Fala da Ajuda ao Brasil," *O Estado de São Paulo*, July 9, 1966, p. 2.

NOTES: THE STRUCTURAL DEPENDENCE

15. Lincoln Gordon and E. L. Grommers, *United States Manufacturing Investment in Brazil, 1946-1960* (Boston, Harvard University Graduate School of Business Administration, 1962), pp. 140-41.

16. "O Acôrdo" (agreement to guarantee private investments between the United States of Brazil and the United States of America), published in *Correio da Manhã* (Rio de Janeiro), December 11, 1965, p. 2.

17. Celso Furtado, *Subdesenvolvimento e Estagnação na América Latina* (Rio de Janeiro, Civilização Brasileira, 1966), p. 44.

18. Marshal Humberto de Alencar Castello Branco, speech before the Itamarati (Brazilian Foreign Office), "Presidente Fixa a Política Externa," *Correio da Manhã*, August 1, 1964, p. 10. Italics added.

19. Chancellor Juracy Magalhães, lecture presented at the Itamarati for students of the Institute Rio Branco, "Chanceler Descreve Política Externa," *O Estado de São Paulo*, November 22, 1966, p. 7.

CHAPTER 11

The Ideology of the Government

1. In the same sense proportionately, the tensions between the USSR and Communist China result from the manner in which the former country is formulating and executing the conditions for its own hegemony in relation to other nations in the struggle for progress.

2. Arthur M. Schlesinger, Jr., *A Thousand Days: John F. Kennedy in the White House* (Boston, Houghton Mifflin Co., 1965), p. 352.

3. *Ibid.*, p. 551.

4. *Ibid.*, p. 559.

5. The legislation that regulates the functioning of these institutions was altered in a more or less drastic way between April, 1964, and March, 1967.

6. Humberto de Alencar Castello Branco, *Mensagem ao Congresso Nacional* (Brasília, 1965), p. 31.

7. Humberto de Alencar Castello Branco, inaugural class in the courses of the Higher War College, "Presidente Explica a Política da Revolução," *O Estado de São Paulo,* March 17, 1965, p. 1.

8. Roberto de Oliveira Campos, Economic Coordination and Planning Minister, in a speech at the Nacional Clube, "Campos: Uma Nova Realidade se Descortina," *O Estado de São Paulo,* April 25, 1965, p. 38.

9. Roberto de Oliveira Campos, statement in a Senate session "Campos Fala no Senado da Política Econômica," *O Estado de São Paulo,* September 3, 1964, p. 20.

10. Paulo Egídio, Minister of Industry and Commerce, in an interview, "Egídio Vé Morte de Emprêsas como Exigência do Progresso," *Jornal do Brasil,* August 21, 1966, p. 22. According to Roberto Campos, the facts, as well as denationalization, are inevitable consequences of "change in production scale, greater capital needs, and rapid technological spurt." Roberto de Oliveira Campos, "Balanço Positivo da Cooperação Estrangeira," *O Estado do São Paulo,* December 25, 1966, p. 36.

11. Comment on Decree Law No. 63 altering the custom tariffs in force since 1957. "Tarifas Provocam Forte Impacto," *O Estado de São Paulo,* November 25, 1966, p. 19.

12. President Castello Branco while inaugurating in Manaus the First Meeting of Incentives for Development of Amazónia, "Castelo: Eleições Livres Deram Confiança, a Investidores," *Jornal do Brasil,* December 4, 1966, p. 22.

13. Aníbal Pinto and Osvaldo Sunkel, "Economistas Latino-Americanos nos Países Desenvolvidos," *Revista Civilização Brasileira,* Ano 1, No. 8 (Rio de Janeiro, 1966), pp. 107-20; quotation from pp. 114-15.

NOTES: DICTATORSHIP

CHAPTER 12

Dictatorship

1. Roberto de Oliveira Campos, quoted by Hermano Alves, "Frieza Operacional," *Correio da Manhã* (Rio de Janeiro), January 10, 1965, p. 2.

2. President Castello Branco, inaugural class in the courses of the Higher War College, "Aula Inaugural do Presidente na Escola Superior de Guerra," *O Estado de São Paulo*, March 17, 1965, p. 7.

3. Reference to former Governor Carlos Lacerda.

4. Oliveiros S. Ferreira, "Fim do Subdesenvolvimento," *O Estado de São Paulo*, October 30, 1966, p. 87.

5. Roberto de Abreu Sodré, Governor of the State of São Paulo, in a speech during a dinner given in his honor by the management of the magazine *Boletim Cambial,* "Sodré Hoje com Castelo," *O Estado de São Paulo*, November 9, 1966, p. 4.

6. Ferreira, "Fim do Subdesenvolvimento," p. 87.

7. Fundação Getúlio Vargas, *Conjuntura Econômica: Retrospecto 1963*, Ano XVIII, No. 2 (Rio de Janeiro, 1964), p. 13.

8. José Ermírio de Morais Filho, testimony for "Como Industriais Jovens Vêem a Situação Nacional," *Jornal do Brasil*, April 29, 1962, p. 14.

9. José Luis Moreira de Sousa, *ibid.*

10. Some revelations on the combination of national and foreign interests as well as economic and military (under state control since April, 1964) were proferred by one of the leaders of the coup: Carlos Lacerda, "Anistia e Mudança da Carta," *Jornal da Tarde* (São Paulo), December 21, 1966, p. 4.

11. Rafael Noschese, speech made during the inauguration of the organization, "Instalado na FIESP o Grupo Permanente de Mobilização Industrial," *O Estado de São Paulo*, May 1, 1964, p. 24.

12. Victório Ferraz, President of the Permanent Group for Industrial Mobilization, in a speech given during the group's inauguration, *O Estado de São Paulo*, May 1, 1964, p. 24.

13. Oliveiros S. Ferreira, "O Plebiscito Cotidiano da Grandeza

Nacional," *O Estado de São Paulo,* November 13, 1966, p. 113.

14. Roberto de Oliveira Campos, "Plano do Govêrno Revolucionário," *O Estado de São Paulo,* August 15, 1964, p. 16. Italics in the original.

15. Roberto de Oliveira Campos, in a speech before the Senate on April 2, 1964. Quoted in Paulo Singer, "Ciclos de Conjuntura em Economias Subdesenvolvidas," *Revista Civilização Brasileira,* Ano I, No. 2 (Rio de Janeiro, 1965), pp. 93-111.

16. Roberto de Oliveira Campos, "A Nova Imagem do Trabalhismo," *Digesto Econômico,* Ano XXI, No. 188 (São Paulo, 1966), pp. 8-10; quotation from pp. 8-9. Italics in the original.

17. Discussion of motives for the decree law establishing criteria for the unification of salary adjustments, "Decreto Estabelece Normas Rígidas para Reajustes Salarias," *Fôlha de São Paulo,* August 2, 1966, p. 9.

18. Law regulating the right to strike (Chapter 6: Illegality of Strikes) sanctioned by the President of the Republic on June 1, 1964. "A Íntegra da Lei sôbre Direito de Greve," *O Estado de São Paulo,* June 2, 1964, p. 5.

19. Marshal Humberto de Alencar Castello Branco, "Castelo: Intoleráveis Tentativas Contra-Revolucionárias," *Fôlha de São Paulo,* May 29, 1965, p. 3.

20. *A Constituição Federal e suas Modificações Incorporadas ao Texto* (Amendments, Institutional Acts, and Their Complements), prepared by Osny Duarte Pereira (Rio de Janeiro, Editôra Civilização Brasileira, 1966). *Constituição da Republica dos Estados Unidos do Brasil,* January, 1967.

GLOSSARY

Agreste	rocky zone covered with scrub in the Northeast of Brazil, located between the coastal plain and the sertão.
Caatinga	sparse, thorny vegetation in the arid sertões of the Northeast of Brazil.
Cambio de custo	cost exchange rate.
Clube Militar	Officers' Club, where military commanders meet to discuss and resolve problems.
Coluna Prestes	the long march through Brazil in the 1920s for social and economic reforms, led by Luiz Carlos Prestes, titular and spiritual leader of the Brazilian Communist Party.
Compadre	a relationship between two genetically unrelated individuals which involves their families and implies lifelong friendship and mutual obligations.
Confisco cambial	an artificial exchange rate used for coffee exporters whereby a percentage from the sale was withheld from the exporter and went to the federal government.
Coronelismo	a system of political bossism in a município or administrative subdivision in Brazil.
Estado Nôvo	a corporate state begun in 1937 under Vargas in which the government held wide powers of intervention, especially for economic and social reforms.
Eletrobrás	Brazilian Electric Corporation, the national power monopoly.
Gaúcho	native of the state of Rio Grande do Sul.

GLOSSARY

Getulismo
: policy of social, political, economic, and cultural reforms initiated under Getúlio Vargas.

Hectare
: Brazilian unit of land measure, equal to 10,000 square meters, and equivalent to 2.47 acres.

Integralismo
: fascist movement that emerged in the early days of the Vargas administration led by Plinio Salgado. It was outlawed in 1937, formed again after Vargas' resignation, and was outlawed a second time in 1947.

Mate (erva-mate)
: a leaf from which tea is made, the *Ilex paraguayensis*.

Município
: a Brazilian administrative subdivision of a state, consisting of a city with the surrounding territory.

Mutirão
: a work project done by many men for one who then rewards them with a party.

Palma
: an old measure of length, equal to about 23 centimeters.

Paulista
: a native or resident of the state of São Paulo.

Petebistas
: members of the Brazilian Labor Party (PTB).

Petrobrás
: Brazilian Petroleum Corporation, the national oil monopoly.

Plano Salte
: plan proposed during the administration of Eurico Dutra to develop sanitation, food production, transportation, and power.

Plano Trienal
: plan proposed during the administration of João Goulart in an attempt to return to the nationalist model of economic development.

Programa de Metas
: Target Program, proposed under the administration of Juscelino Kubitschek. It established goals in power development, transportation, agriculture, basic industries, and education.

Promessa de Venda de Cambiais
: exchange contact in which the Bank of Brazil agrees to buy exchange. All exchange transactions must be covered by a Promessa. By this means the Bank of Brazil controls exchange.

Queremismo	movement in 1945 which advocated that Vargas remain in office while a Constituent Assembly was created. Comes from *queremos*, "we want."
Sertão	semi-arid area in the Northeast of Brazil covered with sparse, thorny vegetation.
Socialization of losses	policy under Kubitschek in which the government paid the coffeegrowers for surplus coffee that they did not export in order to maintain the world price.
Tenentismo	radical wing of the military which supported Vargas and Goulart. It was based on an uprising of army officers in 1924 who marched through the interior of Brazil to arouse the people for social and economic reforms (*see* Coluna Prestes). Led by Luiz Carlos Prestes.
Treaty of Tordesillas	agreement in 1494 that divided the world between Spain and Portugal, whereby Brazil was given to Portugal.

ABBREVIATIONS

AP   Popular Action Party (Ação Popular)
BNB   Bank of the Northeast of Brazil (Banco do Nordeste do Brasil)
BNDE   National Economic Development Bank (Banco Nacional do Desenvolvimento Econômico)
CACEX   Office of Foreign Commerce (Carteira de Comércio Exterior)
CGT   General Workers' Confederation (Confederação Geral dos Trabalhadores)
CHEVF   São Francisco Valley Hydroelectric Company (Companhia Hidroeléctrica do Vale do São Francisco)
CSN   National Steel Company (Companhia Nacional Siderúrgica)
DNOCS   National Department of Projects Against Drought (Departmento Nacional das Obras Contra Secas)
ECLA or   Economic Commission for Latin America (Co-
  CEPAL   missão Econômica para a América Latina)
FLN   National Liberation Front (Frente de Liberação Nacional)
FPN   Parliamentary Nationalist Front (Frente Parlamentar Nacionalista)
IBAD   Brazilian Institute for Democratic Action (Instituto Brasileiro de Ação Democrática)
IPES   Institute for Research and Studies in the Social Sciences (Instituto de Pesquisas e Estudos Sociais)
LIDER   Radical Democratic League (Liga Democrática Radical)

ABBREVIATIONS

PAB	Brazilian Auxiliary Patrol (Patrulha Auxilian Brasileira)
PC or PCB	Brazilian Communist Party (Partido Communista Brasileira)
PCdoB	Communist Party of Brazil (Partido Communista do Brasil, Chinese line)
POLOP	Workers' Party (Política Operária)
PSB	Brazilian Socialist Party (Partido Socialista Brasileiro)
PSD	Social Democratic Party (Partido Socialista Democrática)
PTB	Brazilian Labor Party (Partido Trabalhista Brasileiro)
SENAC	National Service of Commercial Apprenticeship (Serviço Nacional de Aprendizagem Comércio)
SENAI	National Service of Industrial Apprenticeship (Serviço Nacional de Aprendizagem Industrial)
SESI	Industrial Social Service (Serviço Social Industrial)
SET	State Office of Wheat or Corn (Service Estadual do Trigo)
SPVEA	Amazon Economic Development Authority (Superintendência do Plano de Valorização da Amazônia)
SUDENE	Northeast Development Authority (Superintendência do Desenvolvimento do Nordeste)
SUMOC	Superintendency of Money and Credit (Superintendência de Moeda e Credito)
UDN	National Democratic Union (União Democrática Nacional)
UNE	National Students' Union (União Nacional dos Estudantes)

BIBLIOGRAPHY

Alves, Hermano. "Frieza Operacional," *Correio da Manhã* (Rio de Janeiro), January 10, 1965.

Andrade, Luiz Carlos de. "Desenvolvimento Regional — Problemas e Perspectivas," *Revista do BNDE,* I No. 2 (Rio de Janeiro, 1964), 87-116.

Arraes, Miguel. *Palavra de Arraes.* Rio de Janeiro, Editôra Civilização Brasileira, 1965.

Baran, Paul A., and Paul M. Sweezy. *Monopoly Capital: An Essay on the American Economic and Political Order.* New York, Monthly Review Press, 1966.

Berle, Adolf A. *Latin America: Diplomacy and Reality.* New York, Harper & Row, for the Council on Foreign Relations, 1962.

Boletín Econômico de América Latina, Vol. VI, No. 2 (Santiago de Chile, October, 1961).

Branco, Humberto de Alencar Castello. "Aula Inaugural do Presidente na Escola Superior de Guerra," *O Estado de São Paulo,* March 17, 1965.

—— "Castelo: Eleições Livres Deram Confiança a Investidores," *Jornal do Brasil,* December 4, 1966.

—— "Castelo: Intoleraveis Tentativas Contra-Revolucionárias," *Fôlha de São Paulo,* May 29, 1965.

—— *Mensagem ao Congresso Nacional.* Brasília, 1965.

—— "Presidente Explica a Política da Revolução," *O Estado de São Paulo,* March 17, 1965.

Branco, Humberto de Alencar Castello, and others. *A Revolução de 31 de Marco.* Rio de Janeiro, Biblioteca do Exército, 1966.

Brookings Institution. *Major Problems of United States Foreign Policy, 1954.* Menasha, Wis., George Banta Publishing Company, 1954.

Calógeras, J. Pandiá. *A Política Monetária do Brasil.* São Paulo,

BIBLIOGRAPHY

Companhia Editôra Nacional, 1960. (First edition in French, 1910.)

Camargo, José Francisco de. *Exodo Rural no Brasil.* Bulletin No. 1, Faculty of Economics and Administration, University of São Paulo, 1957.

Campos, Roberto de Oliveira. "Balanco Positivo da Cooperação Estrangeira," *O Estado de São Paulo,* December 25, 1966.

—— "Campos Fala no Senado da Política Econômica," *O Estado de São Paulo,* September 3, 1964.

—— "Campos: Uma Nova Realidade se Descortina," *O Estado de São Paulo,* April 25, 1965.

—— "A Nova Imagem do Trabalhismo," *Digesto Econômico,* Ano XXI, No. 188 (São Paulo, 1966), pp. 8-10.

—— "Plano do Govêrno Revolucionário," *O Estado de São Paulo,* August 15, 1964.

Carvalho, Orlando M. *Ensaios de Sociologia Eleitoral.* Belo Horizonte, Edição da Revista Brasileira de Estudos Políticos, 1958.

Castello Branco, Humberto de Alencar. *See* Branco, Humberto de Alencar Castello.

Centro de Desenvolvimento Econômico CEPAL-BNDE. *15 Anos de Política Econômica no Brasil.* Rio de Janeiro, CEPAL-BNDE, 1964.

Chang, Pei-kang. *Agriculture and Industrialization.* Cambridge, Mass., Harvard University Press, 1949. Translated as *Agricultura e Industrialización,* by Juan F. Noyola and Edmundo Flores. Mexico, Fondo de Cultura Económico, 1951.

Cohn, Gabriel. "Perspectivas da Esquerda," in *Política e Revolução Social no Brasil,* by O. Ianni, P. Singer, G. Cohn, and F. C. Weffort. Rio de Janeiro, Editôra Civilização Brasilcira, 1965.

A Constituição Federal e suas Modificações Incorporadas ao Texto. Amendments, Institutional Acts, and Their Complements. Prepared by Osny Duarte Pereira. Rio de Janeiro, Editôra Civilização Brasileira, 1966.

Dantas, San Tiago. *Idéias e Rumos para a Revolução Brasileira.* Rio de Janeiro, José Olypio Editôra, 1963.

—— *Política Externa Independente.* Rio de Janeiro, Editôra Civilização Brasileira, 1962.

BIBLIOGRAPHY

Dines, Alberto, Antonio Callado, et al. Os Idos de Março. Rio de Janeiro, José Alvaro Editor, 1964.

Durham, Eunice Ribeiro. "Migração, Trabalho e Familia." Unpublished MS. São Paulo, 1966.

Edwards, Corwin D. "Controle de Mercados e Preços," in A Missão Cooke no Brasil. Rio de Janeiro, Fundação Getúlio Vargas, 1949.

Egídio, Paulo. "Egídio Vê Morte de Emprêsas como Exigência do Progresso," Jornal do Brasil, August 21, 1966.

Ferreira, Oliveiros S. "Fim do Subdesenvolvimento," O Estado de São Paulo, October 30, 1966.

—— As Fôrças Armadas e o Desafio da Revolução. Rio de Janeiro, Edições GRD, 1964.

—— "O Plebiscito Cotidiano da Grandeza Nacional," O Estado de São Paulo, November 13, 1966.

Feuerlein, Willy, and Elizabeth Hannan. Dollars in Latin America. New York, Council on Foreign Relations, 1941. Translated as Dólares en la América Latina. Mexico, Fondo de Cultura Económica, 1944.

Foracchi, Marialice Mencarini. O Estudante e a Transformação da Sociedade Brasileira. São Paulo, Companhia Editôra Nacional, 1965.

Fundação Getúlio Vargas. Conjuntura Econômica, Ano X, No. 12 (Rio de Janeiro, December, 1956).

—— Conjuntura Econômica: Retrospecto 1963, Ano XVIII, No. 2 (Rio de Janeiro, 1964).

Furtado, Celso. Dialética do Desenvolvimento. Rio de Janeiro, Editôra Fundo de Cultura, 1964.

—— Formação Econômica do Brasil. Rio de Janeiro, Editôra Fundo de Cultura, 1959.

—— A Operação Nordeste. Rio de Janeiro, Instituto Superior de Estudos Brasileiro, 1959.

—— Subdesenvolvimento e Estagnação na América Latina. Rio de Janeiro, Editôra Civilização Brasileira, 1966.

Gordon, Lincoln, and E. L. Grommers. United States Manufacturing Investment in Brazil, 1946-1960. Boston, Harvard University Graduate School of Business Administration, 1962.

BIBLIOGRAPHY

Goulart, João. *Desenvolvimento e Independência.* Brasília, Serviço Gráfico do IBGE, 1962.

—— *Mensagem ao Congresso Nacional.* Brasília, 1963.

—— *Mensagem ao Congresso Nacional.* Brasília, 1964.

Gramsci, Antonio. *Concepção Dialética da História.* Trans. Carlos Nelson Coutinho. Rio de Janeiro, Editôra Civilização Brasileira, 1966.

Guimarães, Alberto Passos. *Inflação e Monopólio no Brasil.* Rio de Janeiro, Editôra Civilização Brasileira, 1963.

Henriques, Affonso. *Ascensão e Queda de Getúlio Vargas.* 3 vols. Rio de Janeiro, Record, 1966.

Ianni, Octavio. *Estado e Capitalismo.* Rio de Janeiro, Editôra Civilização Brasileira, 1965.

Ianni, Octavio, Paulo Singer, Gabriel Cohn, and Francisco C. Weffort. *Política e Revolução Social no Brasil.* Rio de Janeiro, Editôra Civilização Brasileira, 1965.

Instituto Brasileiro de Geografia e Estatística. *Anuário Estatístico do Brasil.* Rio de Janeiro, IBGE, 1965.

—— *Produção Industrial Brasileira.* Rio de Janeiro, IBGE, 1958.

Jobim, J. *Brazil in the Making.* New York, The Macmillan Co., 1943.

Julião, Francisco. *Que São as Ligas Camponesas.* Rio de Janeiro, Editôra Civilização Brasileira, 1962.

Kubitschek de Oliveira, Juscelino. *Mensagem ao Congresso Nacional.* Rio de Janeiro, 1957.

—— *Mensagem ao Congresso Nacional.* Rio de Janeiro, 1959.

—— *Mensagem ao Congresso Nacional.* Rio de Janeiro, 1960.

Kuznets, Simon. Modern Economic Growth. New Haven, Yale University Press, 1966.

Labini, Paolo Sylos. *Oligopólio y Progresso Técnico.* Trans. Enrique Irazoqui. Barcelona, Ediciones Oikos-Tau, 1965.

Lacerda, Carlos. "Anistia e Mudança da Carta," *Jornal da Tarde* (São Paulo), December 21, 1966.

Leite, Antônio Dias. *Caminhos do Desenvolvimento.* Rio de Janeiro, Zahar Editores, 1966.

Lieuwen, Edwin. *Generals vs. Presidents: Neomilitarism in Latin America.* New York, Frederick A. Praeger, 1965.

—— *U.S. Policy in Latin America.* New York, Frederick A. Praeger, 1965.

Lopes, Juarez Rubens Brandão. "Desenvolvimento e Mudança Social (Formação da Sociedade Urbano-Industrial no Brasil)." Unpublished MS. São Paulo, 1966.

—— *Sociedade Industrial no Brasil.* São Paulo, Difusão Européia do Livro, 1964.

Manchester, Alan K. *British Preeminence in Brazil, Its Rise and Decline: A Study in European Expansion.* Chapel Hill, University of North Carolina Press, 1933.

Matthews, Herbert L., ed. *The United States and Latin America.* The American Assembly, Columbia University, New York, 1959.

Memorial dos Coronéis, in Oliveiros S. Ferreira, *As Fôrças Armadas e o Desafio da Revolução* (Rio de Janeiro, Edições GRD, 1964), pp. 122-29.

Miglioli, Jorge. *Como São Feitas as Greves no Brasil.* Rio de Janeiro, Editôra Civilização Brasileira, 1963.

Ministério do Planejamento e Coordenação Econômica. *Programa de Ação Econômica do Govêrno, 1964-1966.* Documentos EPEA, No. 1 (Rio de Janeiro, November, 1964).

Moura, Aristoteles. *Capitais Estrangeiros no Brasil.* São Paulo, Editôra Brasiliense, 1959.

Normano, J. F. *Evolução Econômica do Brasil.* 2d ed. São Paulo, Companhia Editôra Nacional, 1945.

—— *A Luta Pela América do Sul.* São Paulo, Editôra Atlas, 1944.

Nunes, Maria Thetis. *Ensino Secundário e Sociedade Brasileira.* Rio de Janeiro, Instituto Superior de Estudos Brasileiros, 1962.

Oliveira, Juscelino Kubitschek de. *See* Kubitschek de Oliveira, Juscelino.

Paiva, Rui Miller, and William H. Nichols. "Estágio do Desenvolvimento Técnico da Agricultura Brasileira," *Revista Brasileira de Economia*, Ano 19, No. 3 (Rio de Janeiro, 1965), pp. 277-63.

Pedreira, Fernando. *Março 31 (Civis e Militares no Processo da Crise Brasileira).* Rio de Janeiro, José Alvaro, Editor, 1964.

Pereira, Luiz. *Trabalho e Desenvolvimento no Brasil.* São Paulo, Difusão Européia do Livro, 1965.

BIBLIOGRAPHY

Petróleo. Parliamentary Documents, Vol. II.

Pinto, Aníbal, and Osvaldo Sunkel. "Economistas Latino-Americanos nos Países Desenvolvidos," *Revista Civilização Brasileira*, Ano I, No. 8 (Rio de Janeiro, 1966).

Pinto, Bilac. *Guerra Revolucionária*. Rio de Janeiro, Forense, July, 1964.

Política Operária, Ano III, No. 5 (Rio de Janeiro, 1963); Ano III, No. 6 (Rio de Janeiro, 1963).

Prado, Caio, Jr. *A Revolução Brasileira*. São Paulo, Editôra Brasiliense, 1966.

Prebish, Raul. *Hacia una Dinámica del Desarrollo Latinoamericano*. Mexico, Fondo de Cultura Económica, 1963.

Presidência da República, *Plano Trienal de Desenvolvimento Econômico e Social (1963-1965)*. Rio de Janeiro, Departamento da Imprensa Nacional, 1963. Attributed to Celso Furtado, then Minister Extraordinary of Planning.

Price, Robert E. "Rural Unionization in Brazil." Unpublished MS. 1964.

Quadros, Jânio. "Brazil's New Foreign Policy," *Foreign Affairs*, XL, No. 1 (October, 1961), 19-27.

—— *Mensagem ao Congresso Nacional*. Brasília, 1961.

Queiroz, Maurício Vinhas de. "Os Grupos Multibilionários," *Revista do Instituto de Ciências Sociais*, II, No. 1 (Rio de Janeiro, 1965), 47-77.

Quem Controla o Que. 3d edition of *O Capital Estrangeiro no Brasil*. Edited by Robert Gongeard, Benedito Ribeiro, Regina Lorch, and Elisabeth Banas. 2 vols. São Paulo, Editôra Banas S/A, 1961.

Resolução Política da Convenção Nacional dos Comunistas. Rio de Janeiro, 1961.

Revista Brasileira de Economia, Ano 17, No. 1 (Rio de Janeiro, March, 1963).

Revista de Estudos Sócio-Econômicos. São Paulo, Departamento Intersindical de Estatística e Estudos Sócio-Econômicos, January, 1962.

BIBLIOGRAPHY

Rijken van Olst, Henry. "Desarrollo Económico y Cooperación en América Latina," in Jan Tinbergen, *Hacia Una Economia Mundial.* Trans. Anna M. Cabré. Barcelona, Ediciones de Occidente, 1965.

Rodrigues, Leôncio Martins. *Conflito Industrial e Sindicalismo no Brasil.* São Paulo, Difusão Européia do Livro, 1966.

Schilling, Paulo. *Crise Econômica no Rio Grande do Sul.* Pôrto Alegre, Difusão de Cultura Técnica, 1961.

—— *Trigo.* Rio de Janeiro, Instituto Superior de Estudos Brasileiros, 1959.

Schlesinger, Arthur M., Jr. *A Thousand Days: John F. Kennedy in the White House.* Boston, Houghton Mifflin Co., 1965.

Silva, Golbery do Couto e. *Aspectos Geopolíticos do Brasil.* Rio de Janeiro, Biblioteca do Exército, 1957.

Simonsen, Roberto C. *A Evolução Industrial do Brasil.* São Paulo, 1939.

Singer, Paulo. "Ciclos de Conjuntura em Economias Subdesenvolvidas," *Revista Civilização Brasileira,* Ano I, No. 2 (Rio de Janeiro, 1965), pp. 93-111.

—— "A Política das Classes Dominantes," in *Política e Revolução Social no Brasil,* by O. Ianni, P. Singer, G. Cohn, and F. C. Weffort. Rio de Janeiro, Editôra Civilização Brasileira, 1965.

Soares, Gláucio Ary Dillon. "As Bases Ideológicas do Lacerdismo," *Revista Civilização Brasileira,* Ano I, No. 4 (Rio de Janeiro, 1965).

Sodré, Nelson Werneck. *Formação Histórica do Brasil.* São Paulo, Editôra Brasiliense, 1962.

Souza, Carlos Inglez de. *A Anarchia Monetária e suas Conseqüências.* São Paulo, Editôra Monteiro Lobato, 1924.

Telles, Jover. *O Movimento Sindical no Brasil.* Rio de Janeiro, Editorial Vitória, 1962.

União Nacional dos Estudantes. *Constituição.* Rio de Janeiro, 1963.

—— *Movimento* (periodical), No. 12 (Rio de Janeiro, 1963).

United Nations. *El Financiamento Externo de America Latina.* New York, United Nations, 1964.

233

BIBLIOGRAPHY

—— *Las Inversiones Extranjeras en America Latina.* New York, United Nations, 1955.

Vargas, Getúlio. "Carta Testamento," in Nelson Werneck Sodré, *Formação Histórica do Brasil,* pp. 412-13. São Paulo, Editôra Brasiliense, 1962.

—— *As Diretrizes da Nova Política do Brasil.* Rio de Janeiro, José Olympio Editôra, 1942.

—— *Mensagem ao Congresso Nacional.* Rio de Janeiro, 1951.

—— *A Política Trabalhista no Brasil.* Rio de Janeiro, José Olympio Editôra, 1950.

Vianna, Oliveira. *O Ocaso do Império.* 2d ed. São Paulo, Comp. Melhoramentos de São Paulo, São Paulo, n.d. (Written in 1925.)

Victor, Mario. *5 Anos que Abalaram o Brasil.* Rio de Janeiro, Editôra Civilização Brasileira, 1965.

Vinhas, Moisés. *Operários e Camponeses na Revolução Brasileira.* São Paulo, Editôra Fulgor, 1963.

Weffort, Francisco C. "Política de Massas," in *Política e Revolução Social no Brasil,* by O. Ianni, P. Singer, G. Cohn, and F. C. Weffort. Rio de Janeiro, Editôra Civilização Brasileira, 1965.

—— "Raízes Sociais do Populismo em São Paulo," *Revista Civilização Brasileira,* Ano I, No. 2 (Rio de Janeiro, 1965).

Young, Jordan. "Military Aspects of the 1930 Brazilian Revolution," *Hispanic American Historical Review,* Vol. XLIV, No. 2 (May, 1964).

INDEX

Abbink Mission (1949), 120
Advertising, 129
Afonso, Almino, 103
Agrarian society: relationships with industrial society, 30 ff., 36 ff.; agricultural personnel, 34 *(table)*, 35; colonial pattern in, 37; political organization among workers, 38; problems of reform, 39 ff.; hegemony of, implied in export model, 47; antagonisms between large landowners and workers, 67 ff.; social and class relationships, 72 ff.
Agreement to guarantee private investments (U.S.-Brazil, 1965), 167
Agreste, 42, 221
Agricultural and Cattle-raising Society of Planters of Pernambuco, 82
Agricultural productivity: indices of, 25 *(table)*; vs. industrial productivity, 31; modernization techniques, 33, 35; personnel, tractors, and plows, 34 *(table); see also* Productivity
Agricultural products: export of, 10 ff., 31
Agricultural worker: per capita income, 55 *(table);* role of, 68 ff., 69 *(table);* types of, 70 *(table);* political attitudes, 72 ff.; proletarianization of, 75, 82
Agricultural Workers' Union of Brazil (ULTAB), 82
Agriculture: principal regions, 36
Alliance for Progress, 160, 167
Amazon Economic Development Authority (SPVEA), 26, 41
AP, *see* Popular Action Party
Argentina: U.S. attitude toward, 165
Arraes, Miguel, 77, 78, 103; quoted, 78-80, 82

Associate development model: as stage in industrialization, 22 ff.
Assurance Crédit de France, 24
Authoritarianism, 127, 193
Automobile industry, 23, 121, 155
Autonomy: attainment of, 3, 116 ff.; of political and military power, 133, 165; development of capitalist, 150 ff., 152 *(table)*

Bank of the Northeast of Brazil (BNB), 26, 41
Bankruptcy, 177
Barata, Agildo, 87
Barbosa, J. C. Horta: quoted, 135
Barros, Ademar de, 94, 127, 129
Belo Horizonte, 29, 127
Belo Horizonte, Declaration of (1961): cited, 84
Berle, Adolf A., 160; quoted, 164-65
Bevilacqua, Pery Constant, 142; confidential document by, cited, 138-40
BNB, *see* Bank of the Northeast of Brazil
BNDE, *see* National Economic Development Bank
Borghi, Hugo, 94
Bourgeoisie: power held by, during period of export model, 48; support of Left accepted by, 88, 103; as reformers, 114-15; leadership in rule of the masses, 198
Branco, Humberto de Alencar Castello, 23; "Confidential Instructions," cited, 136-38; administration of, 165, 167, 172 ff.; quoted, 168-69, 172-73, 175, 178-79, 183, 193-94
Brazil: dilemmas caused by varying developmental models 7; history of, as function of history of capitalism, 17;

235

INDEX

Brazil *(Continued)*
structural dependency, 202 ff.
Brazilian Auxiliary Patrol (PAB), 121
Brazilian Electric Corporation, *see*
Eletrobrás
Brazilian Institute for Democratic
Action (IBAD), 78, 121, 185
Brazilian Labor Party (PTB), 59, 78,
101, 103, 161
Brazilian Petroleum Company, *see*
Petrobrás
Brazilian Socialist Party (PSB), 59, 77,
101, 103
Brizolla, Leonel, 94, 103, 112
Brookings Institution: cited, 163-64
Bureaucracy, civil and military:
expansion of, 128, 131
Businessmen: participation in politics,
184 ff.

Caatinga, 42, 221
Camargo, José Francisco de: quoted, 32
Campos, Roberto de Oliveira, 179;
quoted, 174-75, 176, 183, 188-90
Cane cultivation, 76-77, 79
Capital: industrial, 13, 32; agricultural,
20, 32; concentration and centraliza-
tion of, 170; *see also* Foreign capital;
Industrialization
Capitalism: international, 13, 14
(table); pioneer vs. mature, 173 ff.
Carvalho, Orlando M.: quoted, 58-59
Castro, Fidel, 143, 164
Catholic Church: political affiliations,
78
CGT, *see* General Workers' Con-
federation
Chang, Pei-kang: quoted, 31, 40-41
CHEVF, *see* São Francisco Valley
Hydroelectric Company
Children: in rural society, 71
Christian Democrat Party (PDC), 59
Class consciousness, 111
Clube Militar, 103, 221
Coffee crop: international commercial-
ization of, 47

Coffeegrowing: as predominant productive activity, 18 ff.
Coffee planter: economic influence of,
11
Cold war: consequences of, 147
Colonial economy: as stage in industrial development, 17 ff.; agrarian
civilization in, 70
Colonies: effect of international crises
on, 13 ff.
Commerce and business: indices of
productivity, 25 *(table)*; expansion
of, in relation to growth of middle
class, 128
Communication, *see* Transportation
and communication
Communist Party (PC), 78, 87 ff.,
99 ff.; declarations of, cited, 99-100,
101-2; Russian line and Chinese line
in Brazil, 106
Composite Commission of the
Uruguay-Paraguay Basin, 41
Conference of Producers of Brazil
(Teresopolis, 1945), 160
"Confidential Instructions from
General Castello Branco": cited, 136-
38
Confisco cambial, 31, 221
Conflict: principle of, 111
Consolidação das Leis do Trabalho, see
Labor legislation
Constituent Assembly (1964), 136-38
Constitution of 1946, 58
Constitution of 1967, 195
Consumption: "demonstration effect"
as mechanism for, 129
CONTAG, *see* National Confedera-
tion of Agricultural Workers
Cooke Mission (1942), 120, 153
Cost of living, 54, 56 *(table)*
Coup d'état: defined, 4
Coup d'Etat of 1964, 4, 5, 8; economic
roots, 22, 148 ff.; a politico-military
operation, 119, 120, 123; success of,
127 ff.; new concepts in, 135-36,
143 ff., 165; objectives, 147; as new

stage in U.S.-Latin American relations, 159; ideology of modernization established by, 170, 180; formulation of new power structure and economic policy, 182 ff.; colonial-fascist regime inaugurated by, 202
Coup of November 10, 1937, 89
Coups, 11 (table), 12, 67, 134
Couto e Silva, Golbery do: quoted, 141-42
Craftsmanship: incentives for, 18
Crises, Brazilian: as marking stages of revolution, 10 ff., 11 (table); in coffee market, 18 ff.
Crises, international: Brazilian reaction to, 13 ff.
CSN, see National Steel Company
Cuba: relations with, 121, 171; U.S. attitudes toward, 143-44
Currency: value depreciation by government, 18

Dantas, San Tiago, 103, 114, 119; quoted, 66, 115-16
Decision-making: in hands of dominant class, 114; foreign centers of, 167
Democratization: of Brazilian structure, 4
Depression of 1929, 13, 86
Desenvolvimento e Conjuntura: cited, 154
Development, ideology of, 170
Diplomacy, total: doctrine of, 144, 163
DNOCS, see National Department of Projects Against Drought
Dutra, Eurico Gaspar, 120, 161

Economic Commission for Latin America (ECLA), 20-21
Economic cooperation, hemispheric, 144
Economic development: internationalization model, 6, 8, 22 ff., 149 ff., 152 (table), 162 (table); industrial sector as nucleus for, 17, 116; indices of pro-ductivity, 25 (table), 27 (table); relationship between agriculture and industry, 30 ff.; rule of the masses in nationalist model, 47 ff.; in relation to Coup of 1964, 143, 148 ff.; distribution of foreign capital, 155 (table), 162 (table); role of multinational oligopolies, 166; "Brazilian model," 171; rate of, 186; see also Associate development model; Export model; Import substitution model; Industrialization; Internationalist model; Nationalist model; Socialist model
Economic policies: state as decision-making agent, 20, 24 ff.; of association and internationalization, 23, 62; of Vargas, 59 ff.; crises after 1962, 122, 123; reformulations, 127, 150 ff.; ideology of modernization substituted for ideology of development, 170, 180; doctrine of reversal of expectations, 170, 174 ff., 180, 193; foreign competition and cooperation as desirable variables of, 177; errors in, 180; after Coup of 1964, 182 ff.
Education: growth of, 129, 130 (table)
Edwards, Corwin D.: quoted, 153-54
Egidio, Paulo: quoted, 177-78
Eletrobrás, 26, 63, 221
Empire, Brazilian: military element in fall of, 133
England: international opposition to hegemony of, 14; economic ties with, 150 ff., 152 (table), 162 (table)
Enlightening process, 113 ff.; interruption of, after Coup of 1964, 171 ff., 177
Espírito Santo, 33
Estado de São Paulo (newspaper): cited, 128, 156, 178
Estado Nôvo, 12, 20 ff., 56, 89, 161, 221
Estatuto do Trabalhador Rural, see Rural Worker's Statute (1963)
Export-Import Bank, 24
Export model: period of dominance, 6, 7, 10 ff., 18, 22; in relation to agricul-

INDEX

Export model *(Continued)*
tural sector, 36-37, 47; in conflict
with nationalist model, 67 ff.
Extortion, doctrine of, 60

Federal government, 20, 24 ff., 50, 62,
79
Ferraz, Victório: quoted, 187-88
Ferreira, Oliveiros S.: quoted, 183, 185,
188
Feuerlein, Willy: quoted, 145-46
Filho, José Ermírio de Morais: quoted,
186
Filho, Lelio Piza: quoted, 215
First National Congress of Laborers
and Agricultural Workers (1961),
82-84
FLN, *see* National Liberation Front
Foracchi, Marialice Mencarini: quoted,
109
Foreign capital: obligations of, 6; areas
of investment, public and private, 22;
internationalization as government
policy, 23 ff.; investments of U.S. and
other nations, 151, 152 *(table)*, 162
(table); distribution of, by sector, 155
(table); business-political motives,
166; guarantee of private investments
(1965), 167; *see also* Interdependence
Foreign policies: in relation to international crises, 13 ff.; doctrine of
independent, 48, 65; as manifestation
of populist democracy, 60; reinter-
pretations, 141 ff.; affected by U.S.
security considerations, 162, 164
Foreign relations: industrialization as
result of changes in, 17 ff.; affected
by industrialization model, 38; Left's
reformulation, 88-89; with Cuba, 121;
interrelation between politics and
economics, 159
FPN, *see* Parliamentary Nationalist
Front
Franklin, Benjamin, 183
Furtado, Celso, 18, 78; quoted, 19, 42-
43, 76-77, 116-17, 122-23, 167

General Workers' Confederation
(CGT), 103, 121, 136 ff.
Germany: hegemony of England opposed by, 14, 15; Brazilian neutrality
desired by, 61
Getulismo: elements of, 50, 161, 222; industrialization process during, 57;
Arraes as representative of, 78; left-
ists attracted to, 114; U.S. attitudes
toward, 203; *see also* Vargas, Getúlio
Good Neighbor policy, 159, 160
Gordon, Lincoln: quoted, 166
Goulart, João: government of, 65, 81,
114; plebiscite on behalf of, 101; de-
position of, 104, 127, 140, 141, 142,
146; as director of Labor Ministry,
131; quoted, 66, 92-93, 115
Government sector: indices of produc-
tivity, 25 *(table)*
Gramsci, Antônio: quoted, 111
Grommers, Engelbert L.: quoted, 166
Guanabara, 128
Guevara, Ernesto "Che," 121
Guimarães, Alberto Passos: quoted,
154

Hannan, Elizabeth: quoted, 145-46
Historical events, international: rele-
vant to Brazil, 14 *(table)*
Hoover, Herbert, 142

Ianni, Octavio: quoted, 25-26, 52, 135
IBAD, *see* Brazilian Institute for
Democratic Action
Imperialism, North American, 88
Import substitution model: policies, 6,
7, 20, 21; effect on industrial sector,
24; significance of, 48; adopted by
Left, 88; ended by Coup of 1964, 145
Imports: effect of currency deprecia-
tion on, 19
Income, per capita: in rural and urban
areas, 55 *(table)*
Industrial economy: transition to, 4 ff.;
politico-economic patterns engen-
dered by, 8 ff.; production indices,

by state, 27 *(table)*; agricultural productivity vs. industrial growth, 31; distribution of foreign capital, by sector, 155 *(table)*; national and foreign multimillionaire groups, 157 ff.
Industrialization: stages in, 17 ff., 24, 25 *(table)*; effect of currency depreciation on, 19; as determinant of agrarian change, 37; process and rate of urbanization, 52, 53 *(table)*; relation between cost of living and effective wage during period of, 57; occurrence of strikes, 94-95, 96 *(table)*, 97 *(table)*; productivity based on, 116; expansion of tertiary sector as result of, 128; in Coup of 1964, 145, 148; *see also* Economic development; Migration to urban areas
Industrial society: relationship with agrarian society, 30 ff.; occurrence of strikes, 95, 96 *(table)*, 97 *(table)*
Inflation, 27; as technique for forced savings, 57, 200; impact on middle class, 131
Installment buying, 129
Institute for Research and Studies in the Social Sciences (IPES), 121, 185
Institutional Act (1964), 194; cited, 140
Instituto Mobiliare Italiano, 24
Integralismo, 87, 222
Interdependence: between Latin America and U.S., 8, 147; national and international, 31; foreign capital investments in Brazil, 152 *(table)*, 162 *(table)*; reversal of expectations doctrine as domestic counterpart to, 170 ff., 177, 193; after Coup of 1964, 202 ff.
International Bank for Reconstruction and Development, 23
Internationalist model, 22 ff., 47 ff., 120 ff., 162
Investments, foreign, *see* Foreign capital
IPES, *see* Institute for Research and Studies in the Social Sciences

Jaguaribe, Helio, 202
Johnson, Lyndon B., 141
Julião, Francisco, 77, 78, 81

Kennedy, John F., 103, 104, 141
Kubitschek de Oliveira, Juscelino, 5-6, 22, 38; administration of, 64-65, 111, 145, 156, 161 ff., 202; quoted, 23-24, 91-92
Kuznets, Simon, 214

Labini, Paolo S.: quoted, 153
Labor force: by occupation, 72 *(table)*; distribution in three economic sectors, 130 *(table)*; official policies toward, 191 ff.; *see also* Agricultural worker
Labor legislation: Laws of 1943, 38, 50, 54, 89; for rural areas, 80, 82; concessions in, 94
Labor relations, 51, 73 ff.
Lacerda, Carlos, 127, 129
Latifundia, 39, 68, 88
Latin America: nationalism in, 145; cultural dependence of, 180
Leadership: dilemma of, 182 ff.
Left, the: dilemma of, 86, 94, 109 ff.; reform policies and stratagems, 87 ff.; principles of, 99-100; synthesis of models by, 101 ff.; tactical alliances, 104; creative role, 114; relationship to populist democracy, 199
Leftist organizations, 5, 8, 13, 95
Leite, Antônio Dias, 116; quoted, 117-18, 149
L'Espresso (newspaper): cited, 147
Liberator Party (PL), 59
LIDER, *see* Radical Democratic League
Lieuwen, Edwin: quoted, 141, 144
Loans, foreign, *see* Foreign capital

Magalhães, Juracy: quoted, 169
Manchester, Alan K., 143, 150; quoted, 15-16
Mann, Thomas: quoted, 144, 146

Manufactured goods, 10 ff., 18 ff.

"March of the Family with God for Liberty," 128

Masses, rule of the, 5, 47; as component of nationalist model, 50 ff.; in rural zones, 82; ideology of, 88-94; significance of, 197 ff.; *see also* Populist democracy

Matthews, Herbert L.: quoted, 144-45

Melo, Padre, 78; quoted, 81-82

"Memorial of the Colonels" (1954), 131

Middle class: receptivity to authoritarianism, 127 ff.; *see also* Bourgeoisie

Miglioli, Jorge: quoted, 97-98

Migration to urban areas, 28, 32, 41; causes of, 52 ff.; per capita income in rural vs. urban areas, 55 *(table)*; conditions for, 71

Military, the: role in politics, 133 ff.; hegemony over civil power, 184 ff.; in World War II, 202

Minas Gerais, 33, 48

Ministry of Labor, 51

Mobility, social: principle of, 111

Models, *see* Associate development model; Export model; Import substitution model; Internationalist model; Nationalist model; Socialist model

Modern Art Week (São Paulo, 1922), 113

Modernization, ideology of, 170 ff., 180, 193

Modernization of agricultural techniques, 33, 35

Modernization of economic techniques, 26

Monopolies, national and international, *see* Oligopolies, multinational

Monteiro, Pedro Aurélio Goes: quoted, 188

Morse, Wayne: quoted, 165

National Confederation of Agricultural Workers (CONTAG), 82

National Democratic Union (UDN), 59

National Department of Projects Against Drought (DNOCS), 41

National Economic Development Bank (BNDE), 21, 24, 26, 89

Nationalist model, 5, 6; effect on economic development, 20 ff., 38, 48; rule of the masses in, 47 ff.; doctrine of extortion in, 60; during administrations of Kubitschek and Goulart, 65; in conflict with export model, 67 ff.; leftist interpretation of, 88; as choice of populist democracy, 118 ff.; cycle of achievements, 123; international political and economic systems in crisis during, 150; political basis, 161

National Labor Party (PTN), 59

National Liberation Front (FLN), 103

National Longshoremen's Federation, 97

National Maritime Workers' Federation, 97

National Railway Workers' Federation, 97

National Steel Company (CSN), 26

National Stevedores' Federation, 97

National Students' Union (UNE), 103, 121; program of, cited, 107-8

National Typesetters' Federation, 97

National Warehousemen's Federation, 97

Nichols, William H.: quoted, 36

Nixon, Richard M., 144

Normano, J. F., 143; quoted, 151

Northeast Development Authority, 21, 41, 78, 89

Northeast region, 42, 76 ff.

Noschese, Rafael: quoted, 187

Oligopolies, multinational, 148, 153, 157, 166, 167

"One world" doctrine, 144

Organization of American States, 171

PAB, *see* Brazilian Auxiliary Patrol
Paiva, Rui Miller: quoted, 36
Paraná, 73
Parliamentary Nationalist Front (FPN), 103
Paulistas, 128, 222
PC, *see* Communist Party
PDC, *see* Christian Democrat Party
Peasant Leagues, 77, 81, 103
Pedreira, Fernando: quoted, 114
Permanent Commission for Union Organizations of Guanabara, 97
Permanent Group for Industrial Mobilization, 187
Pernambuco: organization of agricultural workers in, 38; coalitions of parties, 59; social tensions, 73, 79
Perroux, François: quoted, 185
Petebistas, 95, 222
Petrobrás, 21, 26, 62, 63, 89, 135, 161
Petroleum industry, 60, 62, 101, 135
Pinto, Anibal: quoted, 180
Pinto, Bilac: quoted, 140-41
PL, *see* Liberator Party
Planning Advisory Council, 175
Plano Salte, 26, 222
Plano Trienal (1963-65), 26, 65, 119, 201, 222
Plows, use of, 33, 34 *(table)*
Political organizations: patterns of, 5; confrontation of agricultural vs. industrial economy, 11; among agricultural workers, 38, 73 ff., 82; relationship to popular movements, 58; coalitions, 59; in rural areas of Northeast, 77 ff.
Political parties: extinction of, 194
Politics, national: events of 1960-64, 121; connections between populism and middle-class sectors, 127; militarization of, 134, 203; revolutionary events, 171
POLOP, *see* Workers' Party
Popular Action Party (AP), 78, 103, 104
Popular movements: relationship to

political parties, 58
Popular Representation Party (PRP), 59
Population: occupational indices, 69 *(table)*, 72 *(table)*; distribution in rural and urban zones, 130 *(table)*
Populist democracy, 5 ff., 8; effect on industrial development, 20 ff.; Vargas' death statement, 63-64; rule of masses as element of, 88, 94; synthesis of various sectors of society in, 102 ff.; nationalist model as choice of, 118 ff.; termination of, 148; destroyed by Kubitschek administration, 162; under Vargas, 197; collapse of, 199 ff.
Porecatu, 73
"Position of the General Staff": document, cited, 138-40
Power structure, 5; political power of proletariat, 58; coups and revolutions (after 1922), 67 ff.; monolithic, 179; formulation of new, 182
Prado, Caio, Jr., 18; quoted, 110
Prebisch, Raul: quoted, 20-21
Prestes, Luiz Carlos, 87, 138
Prisoners, political: amnesty for, 101, 107
Production, 18 ff., 73 ff.
Productivity: indices of, 25 *(table)*, 27 *(table)*, 56 *(table)*; socialization of process, 39; in a capitalistic economy, 43; of cane fields, 76-77, 79
Profit principle, 182
Programa de Metas, 22, 23, 26, 120, 145, 156, 222
Proletariat: reforms on behalf of, 50; rural-urban composition, 51; political power, 58; agricultural, 75, 82; position of, after Coup of 1964, 188 ff.
Promessa de Venda de Cambiais, 156, 222
PRP, *see* Popular Representation Party
Pruffer, Kurt Max: quoted, 61
PSB, *see* Brazilian Socialist Party
PSD, *see* Social Democratic Party
PSP, *see* Social Progressive Party

INDEX

PTB, *see* Brazilian Labor Party
PTN, *see* National Labor Party
Punta del Este Charter (1951), 103-4

Quadros, Jânio: administration of, 13, 59, 65, 114, 119, 129; ideology, 94; resignation, 112, 121; middle-class acceptance of, 127; quoted, 60, 65-66
Queiroz, Maurício Vinhas de: quoted, 157-59
Queremismo movement (1945), 160, 223

Radical Democratic League (LIDER), 121
Reform: goals and means, 41 ff.; agrarian, 82; Leftist policies and stratagems, 87 ff.; role of bourgeoisie, 115
Rents: indices of productivity, 25 *(table)*
Resocialization, process of, 52
Reversal of expectations, doctrine of, 170, 174 ff., 180, 193
Revolution: Marxist-Leninist theory of, 104, 110
Revolution of 1930, 7, 20 ff., 78
Revolutions: during 1922-64, 11 *(table)*, 67
Rice production, 33, 35
Rijken van Olst, Henry, 116; quoted, 117
Rio de Janeiro (city), 29; real minimum salary in, 57 *(table)*; demonstration, 128
Rio de Janeiro (state): interdependence between industrial and agricultural sectors delineated in, 33; urban acceptance of authoritarian solutions, 127
Rio Grande do Sul, 33, 35
Rockefeller, Nelson, 159
Rodrigues, Leôncio Martins: quoted, 95
Roosevelt, Franklin D., 104
Ruptures, politico-economic, 3 ff.; internal and external nature of, 10 ff., 11 *(table)*; international occurrences, 13, 14 *(table)*; necessity for, 119; incompatibility with foreign interests, 146
Rural Worker's Statute (1963), 38, 40, 51, 81
Russia: in alliance with U.S., 147

Salary, *see* Wages and salaries
Santa Fé do Sul, 73
São Francisco Valley Company, 26, 41
São Francisco Valley Hydroelectric Company (CHEVF), 41
São Paulo (city): progressive dominance of, 27 *(table)*, 28, 29; "March of the Family," 128
São Paulo (state): interdependence between industrial and agricultural sectors delineated in, 33; bourgeois strength in, 48; social tensions, 73; occurrence of strikes, 96 *(table)*; urban acceptance of authoritarian solutions, 127; minimum salary scales, 133 *(table)*; foreign capital invested in, 178
Schilling, Paulo: quoted, 33-35
Schlesinger, Arthur M., Jr.: quoted, 159, 160-61, 172
Security, national: principle of, 202
Self-image, national: changes in, 113 ff.
Sertão, 42, 223
Service occupations: indices of productivity, 25 *(table)*; expansion of, 128
Simonsen, Roberto C., 18
Soares, Glaucio Ary Dillon, 127
Social change, 37
Social Democratic Party (PSD), 59, 101, 161
Socialist model, 8; identification of, 49; closeness to nationalist model, 120 ff.
Socialization of losses, 18 ff., 223
Socialization of productive process, 39
Social policy: after Coup of 1964, 170
Social Progressive Party (PSP), 59

Social relations: mechanical conception of, 173, 176 ff., 182
Sodré, Roberto de Abreu: quoted, 184-85
Sousa, José Luis Moreira de: quoted, 186
Spoils system, 51
SPVEA, see Amazon Economic Development Authority
Standard Oil of Brazil, 135
Status quo: consolidation of, 182, 193
Steel mills: installation at Volta Redonda, 61, 89, 212
Strikes: occurrence of, 94 ff., 96 (table), 97 (table); legislative regulations, 192
Students: number of, at various educational levels, 130 (table)
Students, university: activities in nationalist and reform movements, 107 ff.
SUDENE, see Northeast Development Authority
Sugar and Alcohol Institute, 79
Sugar production and consumption, 76-77, 79
SUMOC, see Superintendency of Money and Credit
Sunkel, Osvaldo: quoted, 180
Superintendency of Money and Credit (SUMOC), 24, 156; Directive 113, cited, 154-55

Target Program, see Programa de Metas
Távora, Juarez: quoted, 135
Technocratic dictatorship, 8
Technology: associated with multinational business, 6, 148-49
Television sets, 129
Tenentismo movement, 11-12, 87, 88, 223
Teresopolis Economic Charter (1945), 160
Textile workers: participation in strikes, 95

Tractors, use of, 33, 34 (table)
Transportation and communication: indices of productivity, 25 (table); as reform process, 41
Treaty of Tordesillas (1494), 147, 223

UDN, see National Democratic Union
ULTAB, see Agricultural Workers' Union of Brazil
Underdeveloped countries: effect of international crises on, 13 ff.
Underdevelopment: anachronism as characteristic of, 202
UNE, see National Students' Union
Unions, 81, 82, 83 (table); union tax, 51
United Longshoremen of Brazil, 97
United States: leadership in capitalist world, 7, 171; relations with Latin America, 14, 141 ff., 146 ff., 150; financing of steel mills at Volta Redonda, 61; investments in Brazil, 151, 152 (table), 162 (table); security considerations, 162, 164; approval of dictatorship, 201
University of Brasília, 113
Urban areas: per capita income, 55 (table)
Urban-industrial culture: in populist democracy, 5; transition to, 9 ff.; affected by international crises, 14 ff.; social and human dimensions of, 28, 51 ff.; importance of agrarian society in, 69 (table), 70
Urbanization: process and rate of, 52, 53 (table); in Northeast region, 76; expansion of tertiary sector as result of, 128
Urban-rural relationships, 30 ff., 67 ff.

Vargas, Getúlio, 5, 12, 114; deposition of, 11, 120, 160; administration of, 13, 20, 47, 59, 61, 89, 197; death, 62-63, 111, 199; quoted, 59, 62, 63-64, 90-91
Vianna, Oliveira: quoted, 133-34
Volta Redonda: steel mills at, 61, 89, 212

INDEX

Wages and salaries: system of minimum salary, 50, 54; indices of wages, 56 *(table)*; real minimum salary in Rio de Janeiro, 57 *(table)*; of cane worker in Northeast region, 77; alterations in scale, 131, 133 *(table)*; legislative modifications, 192; impact of inflation on, 200

Weber, Max, 174, 176, 179, 183

Weffort, Francisco C., 127

"Western civilization," doctrine of, 165, 187

Wheat production, 35

Women: in rural society, 71

Workers' Party (POLOP), 103, 104; proposals by, cited, 105-7

World War I, 13

World War II: colonies and underdeveloped countries affected by, 13; Russian and U.S. leadership consolidated as result of, 150; Brazilian participation, 202

Young, Jordan: quoted, 16